The
Feeling
Muscle

The

Feeling

*How Felt Emotion Can Help You Sit
with and Outlast Hard Feelings*

Muscle

DR. JENN RAPKIN, ND

ISBN 979-8-218-75574-4 (paperback)

ISBN 979-8-218-75575-1 (ebook)

This publication contains the opinions and ideas of its author. It is intended to provide helpful and informative material on the subject addressed. It is sold with the understanding that the author is not engaged in rendering medical, health, or any other kind of professional services in the book. Readers should consult with their own medical, health, or other professional before adopting any of the suggestions in this book or drawing inferences from it. The author specifically disclaims responsibility for any liability, loss or risk, personal or otherwise, which is incurred as a consequence, directly or indirectly, from the use and application of any of the contents of this book. Some names and identifying characteristics have been changed and some dialogue has been recreated.

Published by A Mind-Body Practice in the United States of America

First printing edition 2025

www.drjennrapkin.com

Cover design: Anze Ban Virant, ABV Atelier Design

Interior book design: Daniel Prescott-Bennett

CONTENTS

Preface   1

PART ONE: **A Problem**   15

Chapter One **Feeling Is the Body's Job**   17

What Is Felt Emotion?   18

Felt Emotion Is Non–Verbal   20

The Different Ways We Experience Emotion   22

Emotions Are Feelings, but We "Feel" More than Just Emotions   25

Getting to Know Our Usual Suspects   27

Body Break   33

There's No Word for It?   33

FRANK: It's the Feeling I Don't Want to Touch   36

Living in Our Heads Rather than Our Bodies   40

And There's Research to Back It Up   44

Body Break   46

We Avoid and Run from Our Felt Emotion   46

Giving Our Felt Emotion a Voice   47

The Body Is Our Feeling Muscle   51

Chapter One Experiential   54

Chapter Two **The Frequent Feeler**   57

Emotional Intelligence and Highly Sensitive People   58

Personality Types and the Feeler Personality   60

The Superpowers and Vulnerabilities of Frequent Feelers   63

Attending to Your Feeling Muscle   66

The Cost of Feeling   67

Body Break   71

Boundaries? Whose Boundaries?

What Are These Boundaries of Which You Speak?   71

LILAH: I Just Know Things   75

The Rewards of a Frequent Feeler Program   79

Chapter Two Experiential   83

Chapter Three **The Body Holds Many Truths**   87

What Is Bodywork and What Does It Look Like?   88

A Personal Experience: It Had Been There All the Time   94

Body Break   96

Is Body Armor Really a Thing?   96

The Breath Is the Intersection of Mind and Body   99

KIRK: It Is the Truth, My Truth   102

Our Felt Emotion Is a Truth   106

Chapter Three Experiential   110

Chapter Four **Thinking vs. Feeling**   113

We Are More than Our Thoughts   114

Our Cognitive Experience of Emotion   116

JULIAN: I Really Do Have a Body After All   118

Messages Can Get in the Way of Feeling   121

Body Break   128

Your Inner Critic vs. Your Neutral Observer   128

BETH: Her Lifelong Inner Critic   132

Your Thoughts Don't Always Have Your Back   136

Chapter Four Experientia   140

Chapter Five **Avoiding, Numbing, and Distracting**   145

We Avoid Things That Cause Us Pain   146

Not Feeling It – Evading Feelings   148

PENNY: I Felt Pain on My Own Terms   152

Body Break   155

Mere Distraction or a Modern-Day Crisis?   155

Chapter Five Experiential   160

PART TWO: **A Solution**   163

Chapter Six **Choosing Mindfulness over Mindlessness**   165

To What and Where Does Your Attention Go?   166

TARA: Maybe I Run from Myself Sometimes   170

Does This Behavior Move You Toward or Away from Yourself?

And What Does That Mean?   174

Body Break   179

The Present Moment Is Fleeting and Ever-changing   180

Emotion Is Meant to Move Through Us   182

What About Unfathomable and Immeasurable Emotional Pain?   186

Chapter Six Experiential   189

Chapter Seven **Riding the Wave of Emotion** 193

Felt Emotions Are Waves 194

The Only Way is Through: Riding the Wave 195

Interfering with the Wave: Stopping vs. Freezing 197

ELLEN: I'm Afraid I Won't Survive the Feeling 200

Pull Yourself Together and Put a Lid on It 204

Opening the Emotional Floodgates 205

Body Break 210

When Nothing Gets Through: An Overfortified Emotional Dam 210

Don't Be Surprised If Emotions Shapeshift 213

Tuning into the Body vs. Hyperfocusing on Feelings 215

Let's Play in the Waves 216

Chapter Seven Experiential 218

Chapter Eight **Welcoming in Feeling** 221

To Feel or Not to Feel 222

WELCOME-ing in Feeling 224

When Feelings Aren't Welcome 226

A Misunderstanding of Tolerating Discomfort 230

Body Break 231

LARS: Raised to Freeze His Feelings 231

Trying to Outrun Our Feelings: You Can Run but You Cannot Hide 236

It Takes Practice! 239

Want an Excuse to Go to the Movies? Or a Rock Concert?
Or an Art Gallery? 243

Chapter Eight Experiential 247

Chapter Nine **Taking Responsibility for Our Feelings**   251

No One Can Do the Feeling for Us   252

Displacing and Dumping Our Feelings on Others   254

Expanding Our Inner Containers   256

LYDIA: It Feels Too Messy   258

Body Break   263

Sometimes We Are Just Not in Control   263

The Fleeting Fix of Discharging Our Feelings vs. Owning Them   265

Undaunted by Emotion   267

We Are Only Human   268

Chapter Nine Experiential   271

Epilogue   275

References   279

PREFACE

I feel my way through each day. When I'm tired, I feel so very heavy. When I'm anxious, my head swirls, my neck aches, and my body buzzes with an edgy energy that threatens to overpower everything else that is going on in that moment. When I am nervous about something, I want to get it over with as fast as possible because I want the discomfort of fearful anticipation to stop. When I feel grief, it feels like a hole opening deep within me, a hole that I might just fall through and not be able to get out of. When I'm with someone who is angry, I know it; I feel it, and I want to run in the opposite direction.

I know the feelings that I don't want to feel will go away eventually. But I can't always trust that. Sometimes, I fear that the feelings will never, ever stop.

I am a naturopathic physician, a bodyworker, a former dancer, and a Frequent Feeler (you will learn more about that term in Chapter Two). I spent the first twenty-five years of my life perfecting the art of ducking, swerving, and hiding from my painful emotions. Paradoxically, I have spent the second twenty-five years of my life learning how to open to and sit with those same hard feelings. And somewhere along the way, it became my passion and my profession to help others feel their hard feelings too.

As a young person, I would numb feelings of inadequacy or overwhelm with food, so that I did not have to feel the discomfort it generated in my body. I would hold my breath when I felt fear and anxiety, as it was a habit I developed to protect myself from or push away hard feelings. I would retreat to my room or apartment, and I would avoid friendships and relationships; these behaviors were a way I avoided interaction because interaction caused messy, complicated feelings, and I didn't want to feel messy, complicated feelings.

In my mid-twenties, I had a realization that turned my world on its head. I was anxious, tense, and guarded, and I was exhausted and lonely. I was closed off, not just to my hard feelings, but to the good ones too. I needed help, and I needed guidance. And so, I started a journey that has led me to writing this book. As you will see, the path of my journey starts and ends with the body.

I sought the guidance of therapists and bodyworkers. I had my astrological chart read more than once. I attended workshops in meditation, goal setting, chakras, and mindfulness. I took up running, joined a gym, and enrolled in a kickboxing class. I read loads of mind-body and self-help books. I saw medical doctors, an acupuncturist, a homeopath, a physical therapist, and a rolfer. I did a lot of things, and I felt healthier and stronger. And yet I still felt numb to myself, to my body, and to my feelings.

One profession I hadn't tried was naturopathic medicine. It intrigued me. I couldn't find a naturopath near me at the time, so I decided to become one. Why not, right? It seemed like a good fit, and after all, I was looking for something to do with my life and still searching for something to help me feel more of myself.

My naturopathic education, one that is often misunderstood and misrepresented, was arduous and grueling, but I was exposed to fascinating ideas and effective therapies. Yet I still graduated exhausted, depleted, and numb. I still felt profoundly detached from my life. I knew all the things that would make me healthier, but I struggled to embrace and embody what I knew. One night, leaving my therapist's office, I had an insight. Even with all this knowledge, I was still just talking about my feelings, not feeling them.

One of the gifts of having gone through naturopathic training is that as students we are held to rigorous standards of understanding data and research, while at the same time, we are taught to understand the limitations of medicine. As a result, I came out the other end of my medical training uniquely qualified to understand what science can explain and where we continue to search for answers. Even though I was anxious and fearful within myself, I wasn't afraid to ask hard questions.

Early in my medical career, I began to observe a few very common trends. Patients would struggle to make real and lasting changes in their lives, and they were often derailed from their best intentions and efforts by engaging in mindless, distracting, and unhealthy behaviors. Interestingly, I couldn't help but notice a second trend that felt even more pernicious and sneaky in the way it permeated every aspect of their lives — a hesitancy and reluctance to feel their hard feelings and emotional discomfort.

It turns out the two trends are connected! Simply put, our not wanting to feel hard feelings fuels our desire and willingness to engage in behaviors that don't have our best interest, or rather best health, in mind. Patients who were initially compliant with protocols would easily go back to behaviors that involved avoiding, distracting, and numbing; patients would replace their newly established healthy and mindful habits with more mindless behaviors. To add insult to injury, these habits and distractions can infiltrate their lives and run the gamut from being incidental to problematic to pathological.

So, I asked myself the logical next question. And I kept asking it again and again. HOW CAN I HELP PATIENTS STAY WITH AND GET TO THE OTHER SIDE OF HARD FEELINGS? It was my humble hypothesis that if we could get to the other side of a challenging emotion, we would not need to numb or distract ourselves. And I further extrapolated that outlasting our hard feelings could mean many other positive outcomes: staying in the present moment, making healthy and constructive choices, and finding resilience during difficult times. Asking the question seemed obvious, but the answer was much more elusive. I had to look hard, very hard, at both myself (my choices and behaviors) and my patients (their choices and behaviors). And all roads led me to the body.

To start, I need to introduce the term bodywork (more to come in Chapter Three). If the idea of bodywork is new to you, you are not alone. Bodywork is a catchphrase for techniques and therapies that involve touch, manual manipulation, energy work, personal growth, and/or self-awareness. Maybe you have heard of The Alexander Technique, Myofascial Release, Reiki, or Craniosacral Therapy? This is just a smattering, but what's important to grasp right now is that a key principle of bodywork is that the body is a window to a deeper connection with and awareness of self.

I consider myself a connoisseur of bodywork; I would be hard-pressed to come across a technique that I have not either personally experienced or studied. Early in my career, I would integrate aspects of bodywork into my practice. One of the unique, and frankly awesome, things about being a naturopathic physician is that I can incorporate touch with other mind-body techniques like guided imagery and mindfulness. Using touch combined with self-awareness and dialogue to explore inner experiences gave me a unique insight into the challenges of staying with uncomfortable and hard feelings.

An early clue to the direction I was headed as a physician was that I purchased a massage table instead of an exam table. I would have patients lie, fully clothed, on my table, and together, we would begin to explore, through touch and dialogue, areas of the body where there was tension, numbness, disassociation, and discomfort. It quickly became evident to me that a disconnection or numbing of our bodies accompanies a disconnection and numbing of our emotions — or vice versa, as I would soon understand that it is a "chicken or egg" situation. I stumbled onto the realization that *felt emotion* — our body's experience of emotion — as well as our willingness to sit with and tolerate our felt emotion, play an integral role in outlasting our emotional discomfort. And the body is where it all happens.

Simply put, the body is our "feeling muscle" (you will learn more about this term throughout the book), and like any other muscle, we must exercise it. Bodywork is the path I found to coach, develop, and exercise our feeling muscle. I came to see that the body is a window to understanding how we run away from feelings, and it is a key to learning how to stay with feelings. Whether or not we stay with hard feelings affects all aspects of our lives; it affects our choices, behaviors, and relationships, and it affects how we handle and manage stress, change, and challenge.

In this book, it is my great privilege to present my patients' stories as case studies in each chapter. My patients displayed extraordinary courage and willingness to feel their hard feelings, even when I was still figuring out what it was that I was doing as a bodyworker and physician. It is my patients' beautiful, complex, and brave experiences on my bodywork table that have allowed me to write this book with a deep and exquisite understanding of our human experience.

I dedicate this book to my patients. I have changed names and, at times, genders, created amalgams of different patient experiences, and fictionalized personal details to avoid any recognizable narratives or life stories. Additionally, because the dialogue between my patients and me is so very important to the process, I include dialogue in quotation marks to denote conversation. Please note that the dialogue I present in the case studies is both adjusted and recreated to ensure anonymity and pieced together from my recollection after many years in practice; therefore, the dialogue is admittedly paraphrased.

WHY DOES FEELING HARD FEELINGS MATTER?

As you read this book, you may challenge and question my thesis. You might ask, "Why in the world would I want to feel hard feelings?" In the pages that lie ahead, I will put forth a rationale for the why. That rationale will touch upon the societal epidemic of numbing and distraction; not knowing how to sit with hard feelings makes us susceptible to habits that, at best, take us away from being present in our lives and, at worst, lead us down a path of unhealthy and possibly destructive behaviors. In addition, when we get to know our felt emotion, we can begin to distinguish painful emotion from physical illness to determine whether a feeling needs more of our attention or a visit to the doctor.

We do the hard work of feeling our hard emotions because when we dodge feelings, we run the risk of swallowing and squashing feelings and possibly spilling, spewing, and discharging our feelings onto those closest to us. As I assert in the last chapter, if you don't want to feel your feelings, why would anyone else want to? Ultimately, we are the only ones who can feel our feelings; we cannot enlist someone else to do it for us.

HOW TO USE THIS BOOK

This book is designed to be a self-paced introduction to body-centered concepts and a guide to beginning an everyday practice of staying with uncomfortable and hard feelings, as opposed to engaging in avoidant and numbing behaviors. It is a step-by-step guide to gaining awareness of the ways we hide, avoid, and numb, as well as to opening the door to living differently and feeling more freely.

The Feeling Muscle's purpose is twofold. In Part One, I discuss the importance of feeling our feelings. I hypothesize that our unwillingness or intolerance to stay with painful and difficult emotions is deeply problematic and that this intolerance is feeding our eagerness to distract and numb ourselves with the plethora of diversions that exist today. I offer real-life examples of how "the body" is where we can stay to truly feel our toughest feelings. And with the help of my patients' stories and experiences, I test my hypothesis and find connections between outlasting hard feelings and living or reaching a fuller potential of who we are and who we are meant to be.

In Part Two, I show you how to slowly and safely tolerate and outlast feelings that are hard to feel. I put forward distinctive insight into how you may interfere with your emotions and how you might resist feeling yourself through creating body armor (you will learn more about this in Chapter Three). You will learn that an important part of moving toward yourself is a willingness to look at your habits as either mindful or mindless. And if you can do this candidly and with nonjudgment, you gain the very important insight into owning and taking responsibility for your feelings.

I start each chapter with an epigraph from my own struggle and journey toward deeper feeling. When you see italics throughout the book, you will know it is an encounter with my inner experience and my felt emotion. Through writing about and teaching mind-body medicine, I have come to realize that presenting personal experiences in candid and, at times, vulnerable ways makes the material more accessible and relatable. There are great lessons to be taught and learned when we are unguarded and real as opposed to perfect and untouchable.

You will find "Body Breaks" interspersed within each chapter; these are quick moments where you will be asked to take a break from the cognitive endeavor of reading and digesting information, and in contrast, simply "be" in your body. This book is about being in and feeling your body; stopping or pausing and bringing your awareness to your body is vital to this book's process.

Each chapter concludes with opportunities to try guided meditations, connect with your body, ask yourself questions, and reflect in a journal. These exercises are a chance for you to play and engage with the ideas presented in each chapter. In these experiential exercises, you are systematically, mindfully, and with intention beginning a journey toward feeling, toward the body and all its sensations and feelings – and ultimately toward yourself.

It is my great hope that *The Feeling Muscle* will arm you with new skills and a new understanding. With practice, experience, and built confidence, you can trust and know that you are capable of moving through and surviving hard feelings. The ability to experience and tolerate a full palate of emotions, a wealth of feelings, lies in the pages ahead.

HOW TO USE THIS BOOK SAFELY

Because this book is a guide to feeling more deeply and to increasing your tolerance of hard feelings, I must caution those individuals with a history of trauma. There are many effective, evidence-based, and body-centered therapeutic modalities specific to trauma, and I do not present my work in that category, as my work and insights are anecdotal. In my many years of clinical practice, I have worked with patients with complex and traumatic histories, but they were either referred to me by or working with mental health providers and, as a result, armed with significant self-awareness. It is a prerequisite for my working with patients with complex histories that they have been in therapy or are concurrently in therapy with a trauma-informed therapist or mental health professional.

This work awakens feeling, and with awakened feeling can come resurfaced memories and re-experienced trauma (I talk more about this in Chapter Eight). While I do not discourage anyone from reading this book, I do recommend that the book be read in a paced manner; when we welcome in deeper feeling, we can trigger and open up past feelings, and I advise that individuals with a history of trauma have a strong therapeutic support network in place while exploring this work.

While this book advocates for staying with hard emotions, it also emphasizes the importance of honoring and respecting the memories, holdings, and feelings that live within us. At any point, a reader can take a break or a breath and come back to the material at a different time. As I will explain later in the book, we are not always responsible for the things that happen to us, but we are responsible for the feelings that exist within us – because no one else can feel them for us.

In addition, this book is a tool to help individuals stay with and tolerate challenging feelings, not to stay in or tolerate toxic, dangerous, or abusive situations; these are two very different concepts indeed, and this book does not promote staying in or tolerating unhealthy situations or relationships.

PART ONE

A PROBLEM

CHAPTER ONE

FEELING IS THE BODY'S JOB

I have big, powerful feelings. When those feelings feel good, I let them permeate my body. I open myself and my heart to pleasant feelings and welcome them in. When those feelings feel bad, I avoid them and reach for a distraction. I numb myself, or I stuff my feelings somewhere where I won't find them — or rather feel them. Sometimes, I run as far as I can from my feelings because I'm not convinced I will survive them.

So far, I have.

WHAT IS FELT EMOTION?

In day-to-day conversations, the two words *feelings* and *emotion* are often used interchangeably. At first glance, there is nothing of great interest or particular note in the fact that we say "I feel sad, happy, or mad" to describe our emotion. As a bodyworker, however, I glean deeper meaning from the words we choose to use. We feel frustrated, excited, and jealous. We feel loved, lonely, and lost. We feel our emotions in our bodies. And many of us feel them deeply and profoundly.

Each emotion has a distinct physical experience within us, and how each of us experiences emotion varies from person to person. While sadness might feel like a hole in the chest for one individual, it might feel like a heavy cape around the shoulders for another. Fear might feel like sharp needles throughout the body to one person and yet like a frozen, stiff neck to another. Contentment may feel like warmth spreading throughout the abdomen or might feel like a tingle in the left ear (yes, that is how one patient described it to me). Another person may not feel sadness, fear, or contentment in their body at all.

For some of us, felt emotion is part of our daily life. Different emotional experiences visit us on a daily basis, and for some, we navigate and juggle different feelings every hour of every day. But even though we say we feel sad, happy, or mad, those words fail to describe or adequately represent the extent of what we feel inside.

Because the term "emotional intelligence" – how we perceive, express, and manage our emotions – has wider recognition in today's society, we are more likely to accept and acknowledge that a deeper understanding of our emotional life is important and necessary. We are encouraged to talk about and share our feelings, and we are more apt to embrace the notion that managing our emotional responses is integral to healthy and successful relationships. But we don't often discuss what emotions feel like in the body. And subsequently, we don't talk about how very challenging and painful emotions can be to feel or how we struggle to sit with and outlast these difficult feelings.

I recently told an old friend that I was writing a book about feeling emotions in the body. She looked wholly unimpressed and exclaimed, "Well, duh." While there is nothing initially earthshattering in the fact that we feel emotions in the body, I challenge each of us to ask certain questions of ourselves about how we understand and tend to our own emotional experience.

- Are you aware of when you feel emotion in your body?
- Can you attach a certain emotion to a recognizable feeling in your body? Do you know what fear and loneliness feel like in your own body? Or bliss or rejection? Or shame or acceptance?
- Are you aware of when you push away or seek to numb your emotions?
- Are you conscious of when your emotions feel overpowering in your body and do you stay with that overpowering feeling? Or do you turn away from the feeling?

- Do you ever look for a distraction rather than feeling your emotions?

At first glance, felt emotion may seem like an obvious phenomenon. However, it is not part of our mainstream conversation, nor is it a part of our mainstream consciousness. We take certain aspects of our human experience for granted. Consider how we approach breathing; we know we do it and have to do it to stay alive, but we don't spend much time, or frankly, any time, thinking about it. We approach felt emotion much like we do breathing; it is an internal and innate experience that we are raised to believe we have little to no participation in or little to no control over. Therefore, we're not so interested in it.

It is my belief that there is a gaping hole in how we talk about emotions and, in turn, how we approach feeling our emotions. Felt emotion is a profoundly important inner experience that, for some, can take up a significant portion of our day-to-day existence. If we take this inner experience – our felt emotion – for granted, we don't really know it. If we don't name it, acknowledge it, or validate it, we don't name, acknowledge, or validate our human existence in its totality. And perhaps most importantly, if we ignore its existence, we may never learn to sit with and outlast our most challenging feelings.

FELT EMOTION IS NON-VERBAL

In this book, I use the term *felt emotion* to describe the body's inner experience of emotion – the somatic, physical sensations of emotion.

Felt emotion is our non-verbal or pre-verbal experience of emotion; it is felt by the body and within the body.

Felt emotion is...

- The restlessness or jumpiness of impatience
- The gut-punched feeling of loss
- The antsy feeling of excitement
- The tingling feeling of romantic love
- The head-exploding feeling of rage
- The spreading warmth of contentment
- The butterflies in the stomach of anxiety

Felt emotion can accompany an emotional experience, no matter whether that experience is soothing, traumatic, uplifting, or painful. Felt emotion is a tangible and real experience, and it occurs separate from our cognition and intellect. Our human tendency is to attach words, meaning, and narratives to our feelings, much like a mental soundtrack that plays alongside our feelings. However, that soundtrack is incidental and, as we will see, at times, entirely unhelpful. Put simply, felt emotion exists separate from and in the absence of thoughts and words.

While generally not talked about in everyday conversations, the non-verbal experience of the body is acknowledged as an important data point in mind-body medicine. The concept of mindfulness – our present-moment awareness of thoughts, emotions, and bodily sensations – has fostered an interest and curiosity in the non-verbal aspects of our existence. Non-verbal experiences may feel like an anomaly in our modern Western society because attaching narratives (our mental soundtrack) to our day-to-day experiences is ubiquitous. However, there are indeed aspects of our human experience, like our breath, our sensations, and our emotions, that exist separate from thought. To be mindful and to live in the present requires a developed awareness of these quieter parts of ourselves.

THE DIFFERENT WAYS WE EXPERIENCE EMOTION

From a cognitive or intellectual perspective, we can understand who or what makes us sad, why we are sad, and how we respond and manage our sadness. From a behavioral angle, we see what we do when we are sad and how and when we express our sadness. From the vantage point of the body, feeling sad is a present-moment experience and, very possibly, a deep inner experience; we can discern where in the body we feel sadness, what shape and intensity the sadness feels like, and whether we want to stay with the feeling or run from it.

Our emotional experience is complex and multi-faceted. It begins with some event, experience, thought, or feeling that triggers an emotional response. Scientists have identified certain areas of the brain where emotion is generated and processed, including the hippocampus, the amygdala, and the limbic and insular cortex. Different emotions are found to activate different areas of the brain.

The neuroanatomy and neuroscience of emotion is an exciting and growing field today, and while some aspects of how emotion is processed in the brain are yet to be fully understood, we do know that emotion is consciously experienced in a variety of ways. For the purpose of exploring and understanding the concept of *felt emotion*, I have categorized our conscious experience of emotion into three parts.

1. SOMATIC/THE BODY'S EXPERIENCE:

This is felt emotion – our experience of emotion in our bodies and through our bodies. While a racing heart, sweating, and changes in respiration are the most common physical attributes associated with emotion, our felt experience of emotion is much richer and more complex. It includes our "butterflies in the stomach" nervousness, our "head is going to explode" rage, and our "left ear is tingling" contentment.

2. EXPRESSIVE and BEHAVIORAL:

This is our expression, outlet, and release of emotion. Our screams of happiness and frustration, our tears of joy and loss, our punches as we lash out in anger, and our hugs as we show our love. Expression of emotion is not limited to physical acts or processes; we can express emotion through art, music, writing, yoga, dance, and so many other outlets.

3. COGNITIVE:

This is our cognitive, intellectual, or analytical experience of emotion – where we can talk about and create narratives for our feelings, have thoughts about our emotions, and analyze or understand the emotion.

For example, when we say, "I feel sad," multiple things may be going on. We might be having sad thoughts (**cognitive**). We might be expressing our sadness with tears or sobs (**expressive**). We might be feeling a tightness in our chest (**somatic/the body's experience**), while at the same time, we are holding our breath and swallowing back tears (**behavioral**). We might be feeling a deep, wide hole in our chest (**somatic/the body's experience**). We might call a friend to talk about the sadness (**behavioral and cognitive**). Our thoughts might be ruminating on what made us so sad (**cognitive**). We might be journaling as a way to process our sadness in the present moment (**expressive, behavioral, and cognitive**). We might be feeling a burning behind our eyes or a heaviness over our shoulders (**somatic/the body's experience**).

If we look candidly at these three categories, there is no doubt that felt emotion (**somatic/the body's experience**) has gotten the proverbial short end of the stick in terms of recognition. There's a lot of felt emotion in the previous paragraph! Right?

There may be readers right now who are skeptical that felt emotion deserves to have a category unto itself. And I get it because it isn't something we talk or think much about, and there are people who don't feel much emotion in their bodies at all. But many of us do. Admittedly, one of my objectives in writing this book is to make a case for felt emotion to be part of our mainstream consciousness as well as part of our ordinary, and perhaps casual, conversations. I hope to illustrate how prevalent felt emotion is for many of us in our daily lives, and the role it can play in our mental and behavioral health. If we look at the above examples of "feeling sad," our felt emotion is indeed sufficiently represented. Despite the fact that we rarely acknowledge it, it is very much a part of the emotional experience.

EMOTIONS ARE FEELINGS, BUT WE "FEEL" MORE THAN JUST EMOTIONS

Because I use the words *emotion* and *feeling* interchangeably in this book, I want to clarify a few points before moving on. Yes, emotions are feelings; emotions are felt in the body. But the term *feeling* can refer to many more things than just emotion.

We feel many things like...

- The physical pain of illness and injury
- The pleasure and pain of sensations and touch
- The arousal of intimacy
- The temperature of objects and our environment
- The exertion of physical activity
- The textures of physical objects

And I could go on.

But while we easily know the difference between feeling sad and the feeling of wind through our hair, we can't always discern the difference between the physical feelings of emotions and the feelings of illness, muscular pain, or biochemical imbalance. For example, we might feel shaky and lightheaded from low blood sugar and yet feel similarly shaky and lightheaded from nervousness and/or fear. We might have a heavy feeling in our gut from fearful anticipation, and we might have a similar heaviness in our abdomen from gastrointestinal or pelvic dysfunction.

By acknowledging and understanding felt emotion, we can begin to distinguish it from other feelings we have in our body. As we get to know felt emotion, we will begin to see a pattern to it that distinguishes it from other feelings. Felt emotion has an inherent wavelike pattern about it, a waxing and a waning. As we gain self-awareness and become more familiar with our own felt experience of emotion, we will feel more empowered to recognize and differentiate physical feelings within ourselves.

Perhaps you are someone who is fearful of feelings in your body because you automatically assume these feelings equate to something being wrong in or with your body. It makes sense that an individual with hypochondriacal tendencies may find felt emotion alarming, as it may generate fear and worry that a pathology of some sort is afoot. It is not uncommon for emotional pain to be very scary; when we feel pain so profoundly in our bodies, it can be a red flag.

Conversely, the more comfortable we are with our felt emotion, like our anxious butterflies or our sweaty palms, we can use it as helpful information to understand ourselves; rather than being rattled or upended by a feeling of panic, we recognize our panic as a temporary reaction to a situation that will eventually pass.

If we can give validation to our inner emotional experiences, from childhood on, we create the potential for familiarity and comfort with felt emotion, which can actually help us more easily distinguish between emotional feelings and feelings that need medical attention, exploration, and intervention. If we know and recognize "the sinking pit in our stomach" as our felt emotion of nervous anticipation, we understand that it dissipates after we get going on a new activity, and therefore, we can distinguish it from the hard, burning pit in our stomach that hasn't lessened. We will have a better sense of when something needs further investigation.

GETTING TO KNOW OUR USUAL SUSPECTS

When working with students and patients, I often refer to felt emotion as "our usual suspects." I started using this term to help us recognize that felt emotion can visit us often and frequently throughout our lives, even throughout each day. Our usual suspects are feelings that are so familiar to us, they can be easily recognized. Some of our usual suspects accompany highly charged and deeply emotional moments in our lives, while other usual suspects may pop up every day as a nagging but well-known feeling.

Oh, here comes rejection. I know her well. She sneaks in through my lower back and buries herself right between my shoulder blades. Rejection is such a bother. If she's really pissed off, she holds a screw in her hand, and she tightens the screw between my shoulder blades. She might hold the screw in the tightest position for a few minutes, just to really get my attention, especially if she notices me reaching for chocolate; she knows I'm trying my best to avoid her.

The first time I remember meeting rejection was in grade school, when I wasn't given the part I had hoped for in a local dance recital, although I'm sure she had peeked her sneaky self into my consciousness earlier than that.

Rejection visits me from time to time, but I really have her pegged now. I know what to expect when she shows up. I know she tightens that screw at first but then tires herself out. I know that if I stay with her and give her my attention, she gets tired and bored and loosens the screw until she slowly melts away.

Sometimes, our usual suspects show up together – at the same time. Yes, rejection can show up with shame, joy with mirth, anger with disgust, and love with contentment. The idiom "I have mixed feelings" aptly reflects how sometimes our feelings are conflicted, like when we feel love with sadness or gratitude with grief. Our usual suspects like each other's company, and this can make for some very busy and crowded feelings.

I recently saw *Inside Out 2* in the movie theater and was struck by how much the charming, funny, and creative personifications of emotions, like joy, sadness, and anxiety, help normalize our inner experience. *Inside Out 2* finds its main character, Riley, who is no longer a child but rather an adolescent, experiencing new, more complex emotions; while joy, sadness, anger, disgust, and fear were her usual suspects as a child, she is introduced, throughout the movie, to her new teenage emotions — anxiety, embarrassment, envy, ennui, and nostalgia. The movie so brilliantly connects the dots for us that our emotions can feel complex, but they are also recognizable and definable. They are like our own cast of characters that live within us.

And emotions serve a purpose too! I can't tell you how much I loved that an audience full of young people was being entertained while, at the same time, learning that our difficult emotions serve a purpose — anxiety can help us prepare, and fear can protect us. How wonderful that we see that joy can be found again, even after she has been lost for a bit.

All the fully-realized characters of *Inside Out 2* help us name, differentiate, and define the many emotions within us, and they teach us that what may feel like emotional gobbledygook at times, is just our cast of characters — our usual suspects — living together within us and helping us make sense of a remarkable and unpredictable world.

If we can understand that emotions visit us from time to time, we may extrapolate that emotions can be welcomed into our bodies — that we can actually make friends with our usual suspects, even the rough and tumble ones. I got such a kick out of Anxiety in *Inside Out 2*; she was funny, honest, and so relatable. Seeing Anxiety portrayed in such a vulnerable yet humorous way made me kinder to and more accepting of my own anxiety, whenever she decides to show up.

If we can talk about our felt emotion, we expect it. It won't be a surprise. If we are familiar with our felt emotion, it won't take us aback when we feel something brewing or something powerful coming up within the body. When we feel multiple feelings at the same time, we are not surprised because we know our usual suspects like each other's company. We may not like what our feelings are bringing up in our bodies, but if we know we can tolerate them and that they will pass, we may be more open to feeling them.

If we get to know our felt emotion, we will greet it rather than close the door to it. When our felt sadness and felt embarrassment come knocking, we will recognize them. When our felt happiness peeks through the door, we will get excited and open the door wider. When our felt grief plows through every window in the house, we will say, "Oh yeah, I knew she was coming, I just wasn't exactly sure when to expect her."

- Is it possible that we can become so familiar with our felt emotion that it becomes merely a blip when we register it coming? Is it possible that we can be so comfortable with our felt emotion that we just let it in with no resistance — that we let it do its thing, move through our body unimpeded, no big deal?

- What if we were so familiar with our felt emotion and how long it lasts that we know when a new feeling requires a call to the doctor?

- What if we were so familiar with felt emotion, that when unfamiliar or really, really loud emotion enters our bodies, we stop and take note? "What's going on right now? I'm really being moved by something. Let me give this some extra attention. Let me understand what is moving me a bit deeper."

Jamie, a patient whom I had worked with for many years, came into my office one day distracted and rattled. She told me her head was pounding, her stomach was in knots, and she had an intense, restless energy in her chest. Jamie explained to me that while sitting in my waiting room, she had been scrolling through Facebook. She had unexpectedly come across a picture of three of her friends spending the day in New York City — without her.

Jamie understood that she was reeling from feeling left out, and she could articulate that she was feeling rejected and devastated. Interestingly, her ability to label and identify her feelings didn't lessen the discomfort she was feeling in her body. And while there was plenty for Jamie to analyze and reflect on — like why rejection was so triggering for her, whether social media was a healthy endeavor for her, and whether she was looking for friendships in the wrong place – her cognitive understanding of her feelings wasn't going to change the fact that her body was swirling and screaming with felt emotion. Her usual suspects were visiting her, and Jamie knew from experience that they would be hanging around for a bit that afternoon. Barring distracting or numbing herself, Jamie had little choice but to feel what was going on in her body, to stay with her cast of characters until they moved on.

Does Jamie's experience resonate with you? Can you recall a time when your body was swirling or screaming with emotion? If the idea of hanging out with your usual suspects feels strange or silly, you are not alone. But can you, for a moment, ponder the possibility of becoming acquainted with your usual suspects and getting to know them so that you are not surprised or upended by them showing up in your body? Imagine the possibility of becoming familiar, and even comfortable, with your felt emotions so that you can stay with them, tolerate them (even the painful emotions), and resist numbing, distracting, or avoiding the feelings. Consider the possibility.

BODY BREAK

Let's take a quick break from reading. Wherever you
are, can you put the book down for two minutes and feel
your feet. That's all. Feel your feet.

THERE'S NO WORD FOR IT?

It has always struck me as odd, and frankly problematic, that we
don't have one single, concise word in the English language to
denote the non-verbal or pre-verbal phenomenon of felt emotion.

Consider how many phrases, metaphors, and idioms we have for our
felt emotion...

- **From head to toe**: Hotheaded. Coolheaded. Seeing red. Cat's
  got your tongue. Foaming at the mouth. Fed up with it. Keep your
  chin up. Lump in my throat. Choked up. Pain in the neck. Get
  something off my chest. Cold shoulder. Chip on your shoulder.
  Up in arms. Wearing emotions on your sleeve. Need elbow room.
  Heart in hand. Cry your heart out. Heartbroken. Heavy heart. My
  heart sank. Makes my blood boil. My blood runs cold. Butterflies
  in my stomach. A pain in the butt. Weak in the knees. Head over
  heels in love. Sure-footed. Have cold feet.

- **Whole body**: Jumping out of my skin. Having a sinking feeling. Chilling out. Losing your cool. Walking on air. Beside yourself. Bent out of shape. Don't feel like myself. Scared stiff. In high spirits. On edge. Shaken up. Spaced out. Racked with pain. Pull yourself together. Fall to pieces. Cut up about something. On pins and needles.

Phew... and that's just a sampling.

These are all wonderful phrases that we use all the time. They describe, give voice to, and validate our felt emotion. Think for a moment about how often you use these phrases, or similar phrases, yourself. If you use them a lot, you are most likely someone who feels deeply and often. Even if you are using them to describe others, it's safe to assume that you see and understand feeling in others because you experience and recognize felt emotion in yourself.

While there is not a single word to denote felt emotion specifically, terms do exist for the body's felt experience. The term "felt sense" is well known in the fields of psychology and psychotherapy and describes our body's inner sensate experience. In his book *Focusing*, Eugene Gendlin, a psychologist and philosopher, introduced and coined the term "felt sense." He describes felt sense as an "internal bodily awareness" and teaches his readers to use this awareness to get in touch with a "body sense of meaning." (Gendlin 10) Interestingly, Gendlin is very clear that his definition and use of the term felt sense is not referring to emotions. While "emotion is often sharp and clearly felt," felt sense is "vague and murky." (Gendlin 10, 35)

Peter Levine, a biophysicist, psychologist, and author of *Waking the Tiger: Healing Trauma*, utilizes and builds on the idea of felt sense in the development of his body-centered approach called Somatic Experiencing®. Levine's Somatic Experiencing® is a data-driven approach to treating trauma using the body's felt sensations — interoception — to access body memories and experiences trapped in our nervous systems. He describes felt sense as a blending together of "most of the information that forms your experience" and "the experience of being in a living body." (Levine 69) However, like Gendlin, Levine makes a distinction between felt sense and emotions, as Somatic Experiencing® focuses on "a complex array of ever-shifting nuances," not emotions; instead, emotions are "easily recognized and named." (Levine 70)

So, emotions do not fall within the definition of felt sense, yet they are indeed part of our felt experience. When I began writing this book, I searched high and low for a word for our felt emotion. The terms that already exist, like felt sense, embodiment, body awareness, inner knowing, and interoception, all describe aspects of the body's somatic experience, and yet, despite so many phrases and idioms, there is no term to specifically describe the body's inner experience of emotion.

As a result, in this book I use the term *felt emotion*, not because it is a recognizable or established term, but because it best describes what I'm writing about. The term *felt emotion* is clear, relatable, and straightforward, and I like that because felt emotion itself is clear, relatable, and straightforward. Emotions are felt, and they are felt in the body.

Not having a word for our body's experience of emotion says something. It says that felt emotion is not important – it's not worthy of thinking about or being talked about. It's delegated to a figure of speech, but it is not a legitimate experience. And if it's not worthy of being talked about, it's not going to be something we take seriously or see as important.

FRANK: IT'S THE FEELING I DON'T WANT TO TOUCH

Frank was a successful executive in his late forties. He had been in therapy for a number of years as he struggled to come to terms with a childhood history of physical abuse at the hands of his stepfather. Because of his years in therapy, Frank had significant insight into how his childhood trauma had played out in creating rifts in his relationship with his ex-wife and all three of his children.

Frank was aware of an enormous amount of rage that he carried with him and was able to communicate to me that his anger, as well as his closed-off emotions, had contributed to his failed marriage and limited relationships with other people in his life. Interestingly and maybe not so surprisingly, he had had significant success in his professional life.

Frank had come to me specifically for bodywork. After many years of therapy and self-reflection, he was hoping that bodywork might bring him a new and different kind of insight. He had a unique awareness of his own mind-body connection; he intuitively knew that he carried a heaviness in his body that he believed was a remnant of his childhood abuse. I found Frank's intuition that his body was holding on to something from his childhood remarkably insightful.

Except for some aches and stiffness in his joints, Frank was in good health and wanted to dive deeper. In our first bodywork session, we started with a body scan. When I work with someone who has never done bodywork before, I start with my hands on their shoulders for approximately five to ten minutes, just long enough for them to begin to feel my hands and, more importantly, to begin to feel themselves under my hands. I then talk them through a body scan, where I ask them to tighten and then release their toes, moving up the body – ankles, lower legs, upper legs, and so forth.

Frank's first few sessions on the table were very quiet. When I asked him how or what he was feeling in different areas of his body, he either didn't respond or said, "I don't know." On his fourth session, however, Frank came into my office more animated than usual. He was in a terrific mood, as he had had a fruitful meeting with a new client. He was chatty as he got on the table and continued a good-natured conversation for the first few minutes.

As he lay on the table, I gently asked him to slow down and quiet his thoughts. I encouraged him to bring his attention to his breath, as opposed to his thoughts. His breath was as rapid and excited as he was, but as he brought his attention inward and to his breath, he stopped chatting. His breath became noticeably deeper and more regular.

After another few minutes Frank shifted on the table, as if he was trying to get more comfortable. He said, "There's a feeling in my belly, well maybe more like my core, that I feel sometimes. It feels fuzzy." He paused a moment and continued, "Fuzzy, like cloudy. No, just fuzzy."

I asked him to place his hands where he was feeling fuzzy. This allowed me to know exactly what part of his body he was referring to. After Frank placed both his hands just below his belly button, I placed my hands over his hands and repeated some of his words back to him, "You feel fuzzy. In your core."

He didn't answer, and after a few minutes of silence, I asked him if he could feel the part of himself that lay under his hands. Another minute passed, and then he blurted out, "No, I hate the feeling. I don't want to feel it." Frank shifted again, this time with noticeable discomfort. Frank's face grimaced as he said curtly, "I don't want to feel it. I don't want to touch that feeling."

Frank was unpacking a significant amount of self-awareness in those moments on the table. He had identified a place in his body where he had a feeling – a familiar feeling – and it had come and gone throughout his life. Frank identified the feeling as "fuzzy." Additionally, he knew that he didn't want to feel it. Frank could articulate that he didn't want to go near it. "I don't want to touch that feeling."

Paradoxically, by understanding that he didn't want to feel his feeling, Frank was moving toward himself – growing his self-awareness and understanding of himself. When Frank realized, in such a tangible way and with such a tangible feeling in his body, that he was resisting the feeling, it was an opening for deeper work and deeper feeling. During this particular session, Frank did not feel or stay with the feeling. He stayed at a distance and simply acknowledged the truth of his "fuzzy core" for that day.

I would go on to work with Frank on and off for many years. I chose to write about this moment of our work together instead of many other moments of revelation and connection with his body because this was an important introduction to our work together. Frank realized that there were parts of himself that he didn't want to feel and that he would need to bring intention and commitment to this work of deeper feeling.

Remember that Frank has a history of physical abuse. Bodywork has the potential to awaken feelings that are terrifying, painful, or paralyzing. It is vital that Frank, and all of my patients, understand that they can stop or end a session at any moment – that they are in charge. Touch is a very powerful tool, but it must be used with the greatest care and respect. Bodywork must always be approached with patience, thoughtfulness, and reverence, and this is especially the case when patients have experienced abuse and violations involving touch.

Our work together would honor where Frank was on any given day and what he did or didn't want to feel. Frank would go on, on his own timetable (this is important), to feel many things in his body over the years that we worked together – feelings that initially he didn't want to feel. And each time he did, he felt more of himself and in a more profound way.

As we might expect, when Frank allowed himself to feel at a deeper level, it meant feeling both pleasurable feelings and really hard feelings. Frank's hard feelings felt like he was climbing the tallest mountain or wading through the deepest, darkest muck. But in doing so, one small step at a time and in a safe therapeutic space, Frank developed a willingness to move closer to himself, and this, in turn, made space for healthy and meaningful relationships to blossom in his life.

LIVING IN OUR HEADS
RATHER THAN OUR BODIES

Many of us spend way too much time in our heads. And not enough time feeling our bodies. I will repeatedly refer to the phenomenon of "living more in our head than in our body," so it's worth taking a minute to clarify what I mean. If you find yourself prickly or defensive after reading the first two sentences of this paragraph, hang in there with me. I am not passing judgment; rather, I am simply describing a trend that we take note of and explore in mind-body medicine.

When I use the phrase "living in our heads," I'm calling attention to the amount of time we spend absorbed in our thoughts. Our thoughts involve a cognitive process, where we arrange and assign words, narratives, and meanings to our experience. On the other hand, "living in our bodies" is where we experience feelings and sensations; remember felt emotion is non-verbal and pre-verbal. Felt emotion happens without thought.

Feelings, sensations, and emotions occur in our body before and separate from our cognitive experience of them. It is helpful to understand this distinction as you read this book. You may notice that you spend more time thinking and attaching words and narratives to your daily experience, as opposed to staying with your body's non-verbal experiences. Don't get me wrong. Attaching and assigning narratives and meaning to our daily experience is part of being human. It is important and absolutely necessary. But we tend to spend a lot more of our time in this "thinking" space and a lot less time in the "feeling" space.

Making this distinction between thinking and feeling might be new or confusing to some but try thinking about it like this — labeling and using words to describe our felt emotion requires brain power and thought, but the rest of felt emotion is the body's job. The body does the actual feeling; it is our feeling muscle, and it's high time that it gets the credit it deserves.

Psychotherapy is integral and vital in understanding our feelings and how they play out in our everyday choices, behaviors, and lives. No question. No dispute here. But when talking about feelings and emotions, a conversation that involves only the mind, only our thoughts, and only our intellectual understanding and analysis is missing the boat. If we completely leave the body out of the conversation, we lose touch with how feelings are actually experienced.

My interest is always piqued when I hear or read about the importance of "feeling your feelings" in books, conversations, and the media; as a "feelings person" who has radar for the topic, I come across quite a lot of buzz about feeling our feelings in today's popular culture. But the vast majority of the time, the subsequent conversations remain at a cognitive level, involving labeling, verbalizing, sharing, and analyzing feelings. Occasionally, to my great delight, I hear a character in a movie or an individual interviewed on the news describe a somatic emotional experience — felt emotion — and it resonates with me at a deep and authentic level.

To be fair, there are many psychologists and psychotherapists who integrate felt sense and somatic awareness into their work with clients. The body's inner experience is indeed a part of their conversations and exploration with clients and patients and is a powerful tool to spark insight and personal growth. In fact, if you are intrigued by ideas in this book, you may want to find a psychotherapist who integrates body-centered approaches into their therapeutic process.

Understanding the distinction – between thinking and feeling – is the backbone of mind-body medicine. Mind-body medicine is all about bringing us out of our heads and into our bodies, but at the same time integrating all aspects of ourselves into a whole person – a whole person who is present, engaged, and intentional.

When we shift our focus to the body, we begin to notice our inner experience as more than just a busy soundtrack of thoughts. While meditation is often characterized as a mental exercise – quieting, noticing, or stilling our thoughts – it also nurtures a greater awareness of our felt experience as our inner focus explores sensations within the body. Yoga, tai chi, and qigong all promote a deeper connection and experience of the mind-body. When we look through the lens of the Western mindset and see exercising our bodies as solely an act of physical exertion, we lose sight of a real intelligence that exists in the body; by introducing concepts of presence, observation, embodiment, breath awareness, and mindfulness in conjunction with moving our bodies, we broaden our definition and experience of ourselves.

Modalities and techniques such as mindfulness meditation, yoga, guided imagery, and bodywork all involve a greater understanding that we don't exist solely from the neck up and that our bodies are integral to our human experience. We are not just thinking beings;

we breathe, we move, we sing, we feel, we dance, and we emote. We are so beautifully complex. And we are only complete when we exist as a whole person – mind, body, and spirit.

AND THERE'S RESEARCH TO BACK IT UP

While in medical school, I came across the book *Molecules of Emotion: The Science Behind Mind-Body Medicine* by Candace Pert. While my fascination with how our emotions impact our physical health had led me in the direction of naturopathic medicine, it was her groundbreaking book that cemented my specialization in mind-body medicine. Pert, a pharmacologist and neuroscientist, laid the groundwork for a scientific understanding of how emotion exists in and affects our physical bodies.

I was riveted by each page of Pert's book, and each remarkable discovery she made—like the fact that neurotransmitters can attach to receptors all over the body, not just in the brain. That finding shifted formerly held paradigms; Pert had found the scientific evidence that our emotions have a biochemical impact on our physical bodies.

In addition, Pert's research gave insight into the effects of stress on our immune system, laying the foundation for further links to be made between emotional health, a weakened immune system, and cancer. The traditional idea that the mind and the body were separate entities, unrelated to and unaffected by each other, was shattered. Her research demanded that a more holistic approach be brought to medicine, and mind-body medicine answered that call to action.

During my early years in clinical practice, I stumbled across many more books and many more mind-body pioneers who would influence my work. Coming across Jon Kabat-Zinn's *Wherever You Go, There You Are* was transformational for me; his writing gave me permission to explore my own inner experience, which opened a door and created a path for my curiosities and passions. Kabat-Zinn, a molecular biologist, developed Mindfulness-Based Stress Reduction and has been responsible for integrating data-driven evidence of how mindfulness meditation affects our brain, behaviors, and health into mainstream medicine.

As a professor of Mind-Body Medicine, I would assign *The Relaxation Response* by Herbert Benson, M.D. as mandatory reading for my fourth-year naturopathic students. Benson's research on transcendental meditation paved the way for mind-body techniques to be used clinically for hypertension, heart disease, diabetes, autoimmune illnesses, and chronic and stress-related illnesses.

It is paradoxical, however, that the invaluable research and the data-driven evidence of the mind-body connection tend to reinforce the cerebral and intellectual aspects of ourselves. As a society, we want proof, and we demand data. And while proof and data are explicitly necessary, they reinforce society's emphasis on the mind and the intellect. It is contradictory, but while research validates and legitimizes mind-body exploration, the endeavor itself is not solely a cerebral phenomenon – not even close.

BODY BREAK

Let's take a quick break from reading for two to three minutes. Place the book down, and if you are able, stand up slowly. Once standing, gently sway your hips side to side. There is no right or wrong way, just move in a way that is compatible with your body's fitness level and range of motion. It can be the simplest and slightest of movements. That's all. Sway your hips.

WE AVOID AND RUN FROM OUR FELT EMOTION

For some of us, our reality is that we feel our emotions so strongly in the body that, at times, we want to feel anything but that emotion. It is imperative that we understand that our felt emotion (or rather not wanting to feel our felt emotion) plays a significant role in our choices to numb and avoid feeling. For many of us who feel strongly, the minute an unexpected or unwanted felt emotion pops up, we want to run in the other direction. Or numb the feeling with food or substances. Or distract from the feeling with social media, shopping, or video games.

Sometimes, it is the felt emotion that we are avoiding when we are trying to run from our feelings. This concept is worth slowing down a moment to really take in. To fully grasp the contents of this book, it is critical to understand that we avoid and run from hard feelings, and that for some of us, we are running from uncomfortable or painful feelings generated and experienced within the body.

As individuals who feel deeply and profoundly, we inherently know that it is not just our cognitive or intellectual experience of emotion (thoughts, beliefs, narratives) that we want to avoid. It is very often the felt emotion that we don't want to sit with or stay with. We run from our thoughts for sure, but we run from our felt emotion too. For example, we may take a Xanax to try to stop the ruminating thoughts of worry, but we also want the intense burning pain of worry or despair in our abdomen to disappear. Similarly, it is not only our thoughts of sadness or guilt that we may want to avoid or numb, it is the deep pain in our hearts that we recoil from.

But avoiding and running from feelings won't help us get to the other side of a feeling. Numbing and distracting ourselves is antithetical to sitting with hard feelings, and these behaviors take us away from ourselves. As we continue reading, what we will see is that the very thing we run from – our felt emotion – is the thing that can help us find our way back. And our bodies – our feeling muscle – is where we stay with, tolerate, and outlast difficult feelings.

GIVING OUR FELT EMOTION A VOICE

One more distinction and explanation is needed before moving on to the next chapter. Even though felt emotion is a non-verbal, physical inner experience, it can and should have a voice. Now bear with me, as I know this raises an apparent contradiction, especially since I am advocating for us to spend more time in our bodies and less time in our minds.

Consider these two statements about my emotional experience of frustration.

I am so frustrated right now because my husband is not listening to me. I don't feel heard. I don't know if I'm more frustrated because I feel like he is too busy to stop and hear me or that he won't stop what he's doing to hear me. I really need to talk to him about this. (cognitive, behavioral)

Right now, my frustration feels like it is exploding inside me. I feel hard bubbles boiling under my sternum, and I simultaneously feel burning in my throat. My heart is racing too. (body's experience, cognitive)

Both of these statements move our self-awareness and personal insight forward in a constructive way. The first statement gives voice to my emotion. It allows me to label that emotion, find understanding and causation, and identify a need that is not being met. It helps me construct an intentional plan to address the frustration. The second statement also gives voice to my emotion by finding a vocabulary for the physical experience that is occurring in my body in that present moment. Yes, giving our felt emotion a voice and a vocabulary involves cognitive energy, but we are integrating an inner physical experience with a cognitive process. Not only can we talk about our emotions, but we can feel them as non-verbal inner experiences.

Felt emotion deserves to have a voice, a vocabulary, and a rightful place in our conversation. When we welcome felt emotion into the conversation by giving it a vocabulary and a voice, we validate felt emotion. When we give ourselves permission to create our own vocabulary for our felt emotion, we are giving ourselves words to describe what's real inside of us.

A few years back, I worked with Mia, a deep feeler; for a young woman in her early twenties, she had had many years of therapy under her belt. After a few sessions, she asked me why she felt so strongly about the bodywork we were doing together. Before answering, I asked her if she had any thoughts. Mia said, "I don't know, but I know it is important to me."

I told Mia that I thought it might be because she was finally giving her feelings a voice, and that the work we were doing together was helping her create a vocabulary — a vocabulary that was allowing her to express a part of her that she had never been able to express. The fact that Mia had big, powerful feelings was being validated by labeling, acknowledging, and feeling them.

I will never forget how her face lit up, with both agreement and relief. When we validate an individual's felt experience, and we give that experience words, we give shape and life to it. When we feel the wisdom within our bodies knowingly and openly, we give it a rightful existence. And when our feelings are known to us in this recognizable and accepting way, we give ourselves permission to feel them.

Holly, another patient of mine, once looked at me with a combination of tears and amazement and said, "No one has ever asked me what my sadness felt like, you know, like inside me." I knew in that moment the question needed to be asked. Holly went on to give me the most remarkable and in-depth description of what sadness did, indeed, feel like inside her. After she had finished, she realized with noticeable excitement that she now had a new vocabulary that she could speak. Holly could even translate her new sadness language into shame or desperation language, or delight or satisfaction language. That's the funny thing about giving emotion a voice; it can be translated into our many different emotions.

There is often a common thread among my patients when they realize that their vocabulary has expanded, and their felt emotion has a voice.

- Why am I coming to this so late in life? What if I could have had this vocabulary earlier?
- What if someone had helped me realize that I have big, powerful feelings that can overwhelm and overtake my body? And that this is just part of my humanness?
- What if I had been given the tools to stay with those feelings, know that they were normal feelings, and know that I could get to the other side of them?

When we name and describe our felt emotion, we acknowledge, sometimes for the first time, that feelings are felt deep within our bodies. And by understanding that felt emotion is a tangible experience rather than a cognitive experience, we can create a blueprint to stay with these feelings, to tolerate them, to sit with them, and to know them. Sitting with our feelings does not have to be an abstract, difficult-to-grasp idea, instead it can be a tangible, discernible experience.

THE BODY IS OUR FEELING MUSCLE

If you thumb through an anatomy book, you will not find a feeling muscle. Yet, it is the perfect metaphor (and title) for a book that asserts that feeling is the body's job. Remember, the mind can make sense of our feelings, but the body is where feeling happens.

Simply put, the body is our feeling muscle, and felt emotion is the body's emotional vocabulary. Our quick breaths, nervous stomachs, tense jaws, and jumpy nerves are examples of the emotional language the body speaks. And just like how we strengthen our skeletal muscles by working out, we strengthen our feeling muscle by getting to know and listening to our body's emotional vocabulary – its felt emotion.

Our bodies speak to us through our feelings. Our bodies tell us when we are touched deeply by grief and fear – and by love and awe as well. Our bodies tell us when we are having mixed feelings, when more than one of our cast of characters is visiting us at the same time. Our bodies whisper. And our bodies scream. By opening up to our feelings – our usual suspects – we are listening to our body and exercising our feeling muscle. We are respecting our body and the invaluable information it communicates.

If we get in the habit of not listening to our bodies and not feeling our bodies, we run the risk of not hearing our bodies and thus becoming disconnected from our feeling muscle. Think about all the important information that felt emotion can relay. Felt emotion can warn us that we need to take a deeper look at what we are getting into, like when we have a feeling of unease around another person or when we feel physically or emotionally unsafe. Felt emotion can inform us that we need to regroup or rest, like when we are feeling depleted, exhausted, or overwhelmed. Felt emotion allows us to experience euphoric feelings of love, excitement, and happiness. Felt emotion speaks to us, guides us, and teaches us.

This book is about becoming acquainted with our feeling muscle, spending more time in our bodies, and listening to our felt emotion. Through the pages and exercises in the book, our felt emotion can become an important inner data point for each of us. If we become familiar with our body's emotional language, we can begin to tolerate staying with ourselves as opposed to fleeing from and avoiding ourselves. Felt emotion is information about who we are and where we are in any given moment. Felt emotion is indeed our present moment.

Felt emotion is worthy of a front row seat in our conversations about our anxiety and stress, our addictions and harmful behaviors, and our mental and physical health. It's important data for our therapists and doctors to know about us and to ask about. It's a valid topic of conversation to have with our children and our families and friends. If we give felt emotion a seat at the table of our consciousness, it can only add depth to our experiences, our relationships, and our all-important awareness of self.

In the subsequent pages of this book, we will begin to develop and train our feeling muscle, as we learn how to listen to our felt emotion intently and with purpose. We will explore the real possibility of opening to and riding our feelings with confidence, bravery, and trust — knowing that we can get through them. Understanding that felt emotion exists within us gives us a standing chance to stay with and outlast feelings before we run from them.

Maybe we can make feeling our emotions a real "duh," as my good friend would put it — meaning it becomes something we expect, accept, and embrace. We can trust that emotions have a beginning and an end, and we can rely on the data of our lived experience and know that it is indeed possible to get to the other side of a hard feeling.

CHAPTER ONE **EXPERIENTIAL**

I. BODY PLAY: LET'S FIND OUR FEET

Can you find three to five minutes a few times a day for a Body Break? As we slowly, steadily, and with intention spend more time in our bodies, we grow our tolerance for staying with ourselves and with our feelings.

Let's start by playing with our feet a bit. Our feet ground us. Our feet remind us that we are supported by and connected to the earth. Let's play with bringing our attention to our feet.

- **FEEL YOUR FEET.** Maybe you are standing or sitting. Maybe you are wearing socks or shoes, or perhaps you are barefoot. Feel the soles of your feet touching the floor underneath you. Are all ten toes touching the floor? Are your heels touching the floor? Can you wiggle your toes? How much sensation does the bottom of your feet have? Can you feel the texture of the floor, your socks, or your shoes? Do your feet feel tight or held or are your feet relaxed and gently planted on the floor?

- **CAN YOU FEEL YOUR FEET WHILE YOU ARE...** talking, walking, doing the dishes, working at your computer, showering, brushing your teeth? Can you notice that your feet are connected to the ground as you are talking on the phone, shopping for groceries, reading an email, or preparing a meal?

2. BODY SCAN VISUALIZATION

A body scan is one of the first exercises we play with when bringing our awareness to our inner experience, as it is a tangible way to begin to feel our bodies both sequentially and as a whole.

Consider recording your voice slowly reading this visualization (as you read, leave time after each prompt for you to sufficiently explore the guidance); you can play it back after you have found a comfortable place to sit or lie down. Then take a moment to feel your breath move in and out of your body, and...

- Gently wiggle your **toes**. Can you feel them? Are they clenched or relaxed or somewhere in between? Simply notice your toes. Avoid any judgment and resist having any agenda other than noticing or feeling.
- Gently shake your **feet**. Can you feel them? Are they clenched or relaxed or somewhere in between? Simply notice your feet.
- Gently flex and point your **ankles**. Can you feel them? Are they clenched or relaxed or somewhere in between? Simply notice your ankles.
- Then move up your body systematically (adjust all movements to your level of wellness, fitness, and mobility) ... gently shake your **lower legs**, bend and straighten your **knees**, tense and release your **upper legs**, rock your

hips and pelvis back and forth, tense and release your buttocks, breathe into your lower back, gently expand and release your belly, notice your chest as you inhale and exhale, rotate your arms forward and back, wiggle your fingers, tense and release your upper back and shoulders, breathe into your throat and neck, tense and release your face, and turn your head side to side … Can you feel them? Are they clenched or relaxed or somewhere in between? Simply notice. Avoid any judgment and resist having any agenda other than noticing.

3. "RIGHT NOW, I FEEL" PROMPT

Use this statement as a springboard for a journal entry, a painting/picture, a meditation, a poem, a song, a dance, or any form of creative expression.

Right now, I feel (love, rejection, jealousy, bliss, loneliness, success, guilt, amusement, and/or grief) in my body, and it (they) feels like …

CHAPTER TWO

THE FREQUENT FEELER

I am not alone in feeling and experiencing life both profoundly and deeply. And I am not alone in feeling my emotional pain both profoundly and deeply. I did as a child. I did as an adolescent. And I do as an adult. After a breakup, feelings of rejection or heartache felt unbearable. When life proves to be harder or different than I expected, my disappointment is bitter and stinging and overpowering. When one of my children is suffering, my emotional pain is excruciating – a knife-like pain searing straight through me.

It's hard work to feel so deeply. It takes large resources of energy from deep within. It takes a willingness to stay with discomfort and painful felt emotion. As I would learn through the course of my life, it takes courage. And sometimes, we need a little help and guidance along the way.

If you are reading this book, there is a strong chance you are a Frequent Feeler, or perhaps you know one. A Frequent Feeler is a term I have come to use to describe those of us who feel our way through each day. We juggle strong emotions and frequent, familiar feelings within our bodies that threaten to overwhelm or overpower us in any given moment. We also feel joy, love, and excitement in a big, wonderful way. If not for the many Frequent Feelers who found their way to my office and to my bodywork table, I may never have recognized the phenomenon in myself.

Paradoxically, Frequent Feelers are often times frequent "numb"ers, because all that feeling just feels like too much to bear. It is this conundrum that finds Frequent Feelers searching for distractions or avoiding activities, relationships, and experiences that might generate big, hard feelings.

EMOTIONAL INTELLIGENCE AND HIGHLY SENSITIVE PEOPLE

There are a number of concepts that have deeply influenced my work and that have brilliantly brought aspects of our emotional life into both mainstream consciousness and our mainstream conversation. The book *Emotional Intelligence* by Daniel Goleman was key to bringing the concept of emotional intelligence – understanding and managing our emotions – to a wide audience. It was his book that gave me the confidence to dive deeper into my exploration of felt emotion.

Having self-awareness of one's emotions is the ability to recognize emotion as it is occurring within us in real time. Because this self-awareness is a pillar of emotional intelligence, I couldn't help but see our body's experience of emotion as an important part of that intelligence. I wanted to build on the idea that felt emotion is a valid part of our emotional intelligence, because after all and for many of us, it is very much part of our present moment. While Goleman explores how emotional intelligence enhances our lives, including regulating our behaviors, finding deeper motivation, and utilizing empathy to strengthen our relationships, I wanted to learn how our awareness of our body's emotional experience – our feeling muscle – impacts our ability to withstand discomfort and stay present to ourselves.

The Highly Sensitive Person by Elaine Aron is another book that I often recommend to patients. Aron's work gives important and beneficial insight to individuals who are deeply sensitive to stimulation, social interaction, and the emotions of others. Aron details the traits of highly sensitive people, offers strategies for managing states of overarousal, and explores the highly sensitive person's capacity for creativity, empathy, and reading social cues.

As you read this chapter, you will see how the Frequent Feeler personifies and embodies both emotional intelligence and high sensitivity. I'll add insight into these important concepts by exploring emotional intelligence and emotional sensitivity through the lens of the body's experience. An acknowledgment and exploration of the depth, richness, and, yes, discomfort, of our felt emotion enhances our self-awareness, and, additionally, it welcomes the body, not just the mind, into our conversations about our emotional health.

PERSONALITY TYPES AND THE FEELER PERSONALITY

Maybe you are familiar with personality typing. It is used to classify individuals based on personality traits as well as to help individuals gain self-awareness and understanding of their strengths, weaknesses, and needs. Some examples of personality typing that you might recognize are Myers-Briggs, The Enneagram, and StrengthsFinder. Personality typing can offer significant insight into how we operate in, access, and manage the world around us. In addition, the opportunity to learn about and understand these same qualities in our colleagues, friends, and family creates the possibility for deeper, healthier, and more functional relationships.

Once again, I have approached and tried to understand the concepts of personality traits and personality typing through the lens of the body's inner experience – through felt emotion. And in doing so, I am particularly interested in and drawn to the feeler personality. While individuals have varying levels of "feeler" in their personality profiles, some with higher percentages of the "feeler personality traits" may recognize that they navigate an awful lot of felt emotion, day in and day out.

"Feelers" are aware of their own feelings as well as the feelings of others. They are likely to make decisions with others' feelings and reactions in mind, as opposed to their own, and thus they are often people pleasers. They navigate life, however, with a keen and honed intuition. They seek purpose, meaning, and insight; they are deep and soulful.

Let's briefly review how in Chapter One we broke our emotional experience into three categories.

- **Somatic/the body's experience** (feeling emotion in the body)
- **Expressive and behavioral** (expressing emotion and our behaviors surrounding the emotion)
- **Cognitive** (analyzing, talking about, and understanding the emotion)

When we look at personality typing, we see that these different types of emotional experience show up differently in different people. One person's description of an emotional experience can be very different from another's.

For example...

- Some people may be very balanced in all three areas of experiencing emotion – feeling, expressing, and talking about their emotions easily.
- Some people may experience emotion more through their bodies; these people tend to be Frequent Feeler types, but that doesn't mean that these feelers can't express and talk about their feelings.

Some can do so quite handily.

- Some people may have an easier time talking about their feelings than feeling them. Conversely, another person may be a big expresser of emotion, but avoid talking about their feelings

- Some people express emotion fully; they may cry easily when they are sad, scream when they are angry, and screech when they are happy.

- Some people may have an easier time expressing, feeling, and talking about some emotions more than others. For example, they may easily express their sadness, and yet have a harder time expressing, feeling, and talking about their anger. Or vice versa.

Here's my emotional profile…

I am a Frequent Feeler. I am a big feeler of emotion; my feelings are strong and sweeping at times. I consider myself a middle-of-the-road expresser of feelings; even though my kids tell me I cry all the time at movies, I know I can hold in my tears too. I am quite good at expressing joy; I give lots of hugs, I jump up and down on the sidelines of my kids' sporting events, and my step is known to have a skip in it if I'm in a great mood. I express love and gratitude more easily through touch than through words.

I can talk about my feelings to a certain extent, but not in the moment of the feeling. My husband can articulate exactly what he is feeling as he is feeling it – in real time. He's so good at it. Not me. It's maddening to me, frankly, because I have to come back, hours later, after I have had time to understand all that I felt, and fill him in.

I did not learn to talk about my anger and frustration as a kid (and I took in societal messages not to express them much either), and as a result, I allow my anger and resentment to build up. I hate to feel anger. That results in a pressure cooker explosion of my anger and resentment, which is never helpful and is not a healthy or constructive role model for my children.

We all may have a varying degree of "feeler" within us, ranging from very little to all the time. For some of us, learning to observe and understand this aspect of ourselves can explain why we struggle to stay present during hard life stuff. It doesn't feel good to stay with ourselves; in fact, it feels awful at times. Yes, it can be that simple for Frequent Feelers. We feel a lot, and when it feels yucky, we'd rather feel or do something else instead. As I mentioned earlier, this sets us up as frequent "numb"ers.

THE SUPERPOWERS AND VULNERABILITIES OF FREQUENT FEELERS

Frequent Feelers can walk into a work meeting and feel any tension in the room; they feel it in their body as clear as day. They pick up their child from school and can immediately tell if it's been a good day or a bad day, because they feel it. They are in line at the grocery store and can instantly read the dynamic at play; the cashier is annoyed, the customer behind them is in a rush, and the person bagging the groceries is moving slowly; they can read a room or a situation with deft accuracy.

How is it that feelers can read a situation so well? Well, quite simply, they feel it in their body. My fellow Frequent Feelers may be feeling a sense of recognition, relief, validation — or possibly vulnerability or agitation — in their bodies right now.

If you think you are or might know a Frequent Feeler, here are some questions to consider:

- Have you ever left a room because you felt the energy and you just didn't want to be there? Have you ever avoided a situation because you just had a feeling about it?
- Have you ever just known how something was going to play out? Maybe you don't quite know why, but you just know.
- Have you ever ended a friendship or relationship because the feelings around that connection were too heavy or complicated to carry?
- Have you ever had to take a nap after an outing, a party, or an emotional experience because your body or mind was exhausted? Have you ever missed out on an adventure or new experience because you weren't up for all the feeling it would require of you?
- Do you struggle with making decisions or maintaining clear and clean boundaries for yourself, because you feel for everyone involved, not just yourself? Are boundaries difficult for you to keep because you are keenly aware of how others will react or feel about them?

Chances are if you relate to some or many of the above questions, you are a Frequent Feeler, and make no mistake, you have gifts and strengths aplenty, but your superpower does leave you vulnerable at times. It takes energy and deep inner resources to be you. It takes practice to know if what you are feeling is coming from you or from another person; sometimes it is even tougher to distinguish when there is a mix of the two.

It is hard to uphold boundaries as a Frequent Feeler. Despite boundaries being vital and imperative to your health and wellness, you can easily get tangled in feelings of expectation, disappointment, and anger (yours or another person's). This tangled web of feelings can overpower any situation and leave you vulnerable to or paralyzed by all the feeling.

To thrive, we need to be self-aware. If we are unaware of our superpowers and our vulnerabilities, we can get tripped up. Feeling is a vital part of what makes us human, but we must learn to manage and balance all that comes at us. We must tend to our feeling muscle. If we block our feeling because it is too much, we lose a part of ourselves that is essential for health, growth, and prosperity in our lives. If we get completely lost in and overtaken by our feelings, we become exhausted by everyday occurrences and relationships; we risk experiencing burnout, and we can crumble when faced with adversity. If we have no awareness and no tools to manage our own sensitivity, we are simply powerless to the ebbs and flows of our own felt emotion as well as the whims and energy of the feelings of others.

ATTENDING TO YOUR FEELING MUSCLE

If you are a feeler, you depend heavily on your feeling muscle. Your feeling muscle reads a situation, a room, a person, and has an immediate sensation or feeling about it. In the best-case scenario, your feeling muscle is well-developed and toned; you feel out situations, can accurately read where the feelings originate and end, and can maintain clear and clean boundaries between your feelings and others. However, this is rarely the reality for a Frequent Feeler.

Instead, we often see an overworked or overly tense feeling muscle. Our muscle can become overwhelmed by all the various frequencies of feelings coming at us (our own and others'). Consider how we accept that an overworked skeletal muscle needs rest and nourishment to regroup and recover, and we may have firsthand experience that an overworked or misused muscle can be easily injured or damaged. An overburdened or overtaxed feeling muscle occurs when rest and reset are not possible and feeling overtakes and exhausts us.

Feeler personalities run the risk of developing acute or chronic exhaustion from having to take, time and time again, a defensive or guarding stance from and against too much feeling. Having a protective and armored stance for prolonged periods of time leads to an overly tense feeling muscle; just like a tense skeletal muscle is tight, a feeling muscle works hard to manage all the many feelings. A supple and soft feeling muscle would welcome in feelings and allow them to move and pass through us with ease and resilience.

If the burden of so much inner feeling is too heavy, Frequent Feelers run the risk of avoiding and missing out on connection, opportunity, and adventure. The act of both guarding against and avoiding emotional discomfort deters feelers from living a full life with ease and confidence. For Frequent Feelers, feeling is nonnegotiable. It's not a choice we make. It's innate and baked in. It's how we operate in the world.

Comments like "You're too emotional, don't be so sensitive, toughen up, or grow thicker skin" demonstrate the intolerant and judgmental stance that the world at large places upon feelers. This is where we Frequent Feelers must take back our power. We need to view our stupendous and herculean feeling muscle as an underutilized talent and gift, brimming with great potential.

Because society will likely continue to insist that feelers "toughen up," attending to the wellbeing of our feeling muscle is vital. To avoid depletion and exhaustion of the feeling muscle, a feeler must know how to nourish, tone, and refuel it.

THE COST OF FEELING

Navigating life's bumpy roads is often tricky. We don't always see the rough patches ahead. We can't predict all the twists and turns, even though we wish we could. Frequent Feelers, however, do have signposts and a GPS system that can help us proceed either with caution or confidence, depending on the situation.

Jumping right into a situation is not typically common or easy for Frequent Feelers. Because we are taking in so much information that needs to be digested prior to partaking in an experience, we need to take a beat or a breath before diving into something. Whether it is a conversation or an argument, a new opportunity or a familiar experience, or an important decision or quick change of direction, Frequent Feelers require time to check in, no matter how briefly, with their feeling muscle. While this intuitive data collection may be gradual, taking this time helps feelers stay grounded and centered.

Frequent Feelers scan a situation for where their energy will be best spent, where it may be drained, or where it might be wasted. One of my favorite aspects of being a feeler is that it allows me, or maybe forces me, to be efficient; as I have gotten to know my feeling muscle well, I am always on the lookout for where my energy may be wasted or taken advantage of, and how, if possible, I can protect myself. It took me a while to identify how my energy was best replenished, and even if I can't find a source of renewal in any given moment or situation, I do know what I need.

I know I need more sleep than my husband. I know I'm super cranky in the morning if I don't get enough sleep, and my family wisely avoids me until after my morning coffee. Sleep has always been a priority for me, and I make decisions about the structure of my day and my time that ensure that I get enough sleep.

In addition, I know that alone time feeds my soul. Alone! Did I mention that I need to be alone to regroup and recharge? Even if another person is in the house, I'm not truly regrouping and recharging. The possibility of someone walking in on my alone time or a request being screamed from downstairs during my "me" time is not fully replenishing. It's super hard as a mom and it's gotten a tad easier as my kids have gotten older, but I try to squeeze in a bit of alone time every day, or I'm just not at my best.

The greatest strength of feelers is their intuition, but intuition comes at a cost. Frequent Feelers use premium gas to fuel their intuition, and as we know, premium gas is more expensive and harder to find. Friends and families often get frustrated if Frequent Feelers have too many needs or if they don't have enough energy reserves. One of the toughest paradoxes of Frequent Feelers is to hold firm and carve out space for their needs; because feelers feel their loved ones' dissatisfaction, disappointment, and/or impatience with them, they often forego the refueling that they so desperately need.

For Frequent Feelers, the analogy of requiring premium or expensive fuel is important to internalize and remember. Again, the validation and recognition of feelers – both their gifts and their needs, their superpowers and their vulnerabilities – is vital to their ability to thrive. The gifts of intuition are costly, and must be paid for, somehow and somewhere. When we see feelers who are in debt, they are fatigued and stressed out; as Frequent Feelers, part of our job (with the help and understanding of our loved ones) is to find room in our budgets to cover our own operating costs.

What fuel do you need to best attend to your feeling muscle?

- More sleep? More naps? An earlier bedtime? No phones before bed? An occasional morning to sleep in?
- Better quality nutrition? Meditation time? Downtime? Alone/Me time?
- Curling up with a good book? Listening to music? Journaling?
- Travel? Adventure? Meeting a friend for a coffee? A date night with your partner? Trying a new restaurant? A cuddle with your pet?
- A yoga class? Going for a drive? A walk? A run?

We must realize, as we feel our way through our days and weeks and years, that we are operating on a very deep level. There are levels and depths to the information and frequencies that we receive and must make sense of. By nature, Frequent Feelers are deep, soulful individuals whose gifts and needs run equally as deep.

Feelers seek and require both experiences and people who ground their life with meaning and purpose. Feelers operate best when their feet are firmly planted and grounded and yet their hearts are open. We look for opportunities that challenge us and that break us apart. Yes, break us apart – because there is a deep knowing of what makes our lives truly tick; our intuition knows the beauty of growth and transformation, and it realizes that this metamorphosis only comes when we are challenged and tested. As Frequent Feelers, we take up the space we deserve in the world when we fully embrace who we are and what we need.

BODY BREAK

Let's take two to three minutes to check in with our bodies.
Reading about the needs of our feeler personality and
our feeling muscle might have brought up some feelings
in your body. Maybe validation or anxiety? Perhaps fear
or acceptance? Frustration? Restlessness? Contentment?
Take a moment and bring your awareness inward to your
chest and your gut. Are there any feelings or sensations
brewing? Maybe there are, maybe not. Resist judging or
trying to manufacture a feeling. Simply notice. That's all.

BOUNDARIES? WHOSE BOUNDARIES? WHAT ARE THESE BOUNDARIES OF WHICH YOU SPEAK?

Of course, creating boundaries around how we spend our time,
how we spend our energy, and how we define our personal space
is important for everyone to understand and uphold for themselves.
For Frequent Feelers, it is imperative.

As a Frequent Feeler myself, maintaining boundaries has been
and continues to be one of my greatest challenges. Before
understanding both the strengths and weaknesses of my feeler
personality, I had zero insight into why I struggled to tell people

"No," and why I felt so compelled to be a people pleaser, while at the same time avoiding friendships and relationships due to a fear of conflict and confrontation.

Avoiding connection and friendships meant I was less likely to make waves and mistakes. While making mistakes meant disappointing and angering people, making waves meant standing up for myself, speaking my truth, and holding my ground. All of those things ran the risk of putting me in the direct line of fire of another person's disappointment, frustration, and possibly even rage. Yikes! Too many times, I sat with my own internal frustration (yes, my felt frustration) of not being able to voice my truth or of not being heard or validated because I couldn't bear to feel the anger or frustration of another person toward me. It felt utterly intolerable.

I did not learn about the concept of boundaries until early adulthood; I was a late bloomer, so to speak, on the self-awareness front. I can remember having a very difficult time wrapping my head around the concept of boundaries. As Frequent Feelers, realizing that we have the right to establish ground rules around how others respect us – our person, our being, our time, our space, our body – is vitally important. Understanding that maintaining and honoring the boundaries that we establish for ourselves might mean displeasing or, even worse, angering someone, can be very hard for Frequent Feelers.

• Have you ever weighed the pros and cons of feeling your own frustration and disappointment vs. feeling someone else's?

- Have you ever chosen to disappoint or let down yourself, rather than disappoint or let down another person?
- Have you ever made the internal calculation to not be true to yourself or your feelings to spare or protect another's feelings?
- Have you ever apologized for something that was not your fault because you didn't want to face another's disapproval or rage?

If these questions make sense to you and you don't have to think long before answering yes, you are very likely a Frequent Feeler. For a feeler, this reluctance or inability to upset another individual is simply one more example of not being able to sit with the felt emotion that angering someone would evoke. To be clear, there may be times when we would rather tolerate our own emotional discomfort (our felt emotion) than feel another's directed at us. We might choose to acquiesce or please another person and not speak our truth so that we avoid feeling someone else's anger, frustration, or disappointment. It's important to take a moment to let that statement sink in because it may feel poignant or validating, or maybe distressing and defeating, for some.

As a result of a Frequent Feeler's struggle with boundaries, we may pull back from friendships and social connections because avoiding connection is easier than actually maintaining boundaries — boundaries we so desperately need but don't always understand. Ultimately, we may very well have disappointed people in our lives due to our pulling back from a friendship or flat-out avoiding or ending one.

Personally, I have learned to manage the expectations someone might have of me from the start. I borrow from how therapists work with patients – by being very clear about the boundaries of what remains confidential within the therapeutic relationship and what can't be considered privileged due to the health and wellbeing of a client. I have taken to being honest very early in new friendships about what one can expect of my time and energy. While this might seem cold and abrasive in the abstract, I assure you that it has allowed for a better understanding of what I am capable of and why I sometimes back away. Asking someone to respect this part of me opens up a mutual opportunity for a new friend to set a boundary or feel comfortable stating out loud something they need me to know about them.

Boundaries are hard to maintain, especially when we are confronted with not just our own strong feelings but the strong feelings of others. As a bodyworker who utilizes touch with patients, I am constantly confronted with the question of whose feelings am I feeling right now – mine or my patient's? For my first few years in practice, the answer to this question was not clear-cut. I had to work long and hard to distinguish my feelings from the feelings of my patients.

Sometimes, I use imagery to create imaginary bubbles or boundaries around myself and the patient lying on my table. I place feelings in these imaginary bubbles too, and it helps me keep feelings straight. Are these feelings coming from me or my patient? Interestingly, when I started to use this imagery technique in my professional life, I found it helpful in my personal life too (you will find a similar exercise in the experiential section of this chapter). When things started to get messy for me in a disagreement or conflict with a loved one, I could have some clarity around the different feelings that were swirling around me. Were they mine or my friend's, family member's, or partner's? With time, I could begin to distinguish between feelings coming at me versus feelings generated within me. It didn't make tolerating those feelings easier, but it did help me feel less lost or overwhelmed by the tsunami of felt emotion washing over me.

LILAH: I JUST KNOW THINGS

Lilah had suffered from anxiety for years and was currently having trouble controlling her blood pressure despite being on medication. Lilah had come to me to learn relaxation techniques. She was interested in learning more about meditation and wanted to establish a daily meditation practice. She hoped that if she were able to relax better, her blood pressure medications would work better.

Lilah had never married or had children, and she felt that absence in her life deeply. The fact that she did not have her own family often came up in our conversations around her health. She was convinced that her grief about not having had the opportunity to have a family had contributed to her health issues.

Lilah's work was stressful. She was an administrator and juggled an enormous workload. Over the years, her boss had recognized that she was truly gifted at connecting with clients; that, combined with her impeccable work ethic, had led to a lot of promotions and many additional responsibilities. With that recognition had come an increase in her anxiety, and a deeper pain that she had dedicated her life to work, instead of a family. Her numerous comments about the absence of family in her life led me to suspect that she had a deeper intuition about herself and her health.

In one bodywork session, Lilah was having a very difficult time relaxing on the table. Frequent Feelers are often hesitant to tell me when they are really struggling to relax because they feel like there is a "right way" to relax and want to "please" me. Lilah blurted out, "This is so hard for me today. I want to be anywhere else but on this table right now." Then she immediately wanted to take back her words, "I'm sorry. I'm not being a good patient today."

My response to authentic and honest feedback is always, "I'm so glad you can be honest with what you are truly feeling. Let's stay with this." And often I will repeat back their words. "You said this is hard for you, and you wish you were anywhere but here. Can you tell me more about where you are and what you are feeling right now?"

It's not uncommon that patients believe they should act in a certain way, achieve a certain level of deep relaxation, or come to some epiphany while on the table – you know, to be the "perfect" patient. And it is an important part of my job to throw those expectations out the window and establish an authentic openness to and acceptance of the present moment.

Expectations and agendas move us away from the present moment — from our present moment. Beliefs about being "good" or "perfect" or "right" take us away from ourselves. Giving ourselves permission to feel exactly what we are feeling, whether it feels good or not, or right or not, points us in the direction of feeling — it gets us on the path toward ourselves.

Lilah continued, "I can't sit in my own skin right now. I feel like I'm beside myself, not in myself." She continued with restlessness in her voice, "Ugh, and my gut feels like it's on fire." I softly placed my hands on her abdomen and gently encouraged her to stay with the discomfort she was feeling — to stay with her gut feeling.

We were both quiet as she stayed with her feelings for many minutes. I saw her breath move from quick, shallow breaths to deeper, longer ones. And after a few more minutes of silence, she said, "I see from my gut."

I let her words linger in the silence that followed, and then slowly repeated her words back to her, "You see from your gut." After a few more minutes of silence and staying with her feeling, Lilah calmly said, "I just know things." She said this in a more confident and direct manner than usual.

She proceeded to tell me that she knew things about her clients and her coworkers. Her gut would tell her things about herself too. She continued to explain that just then, on the table and staying with her gut feeling, she had had an important insight. It became clear to her that her strict upbringing and her science background in college had taught her not to trust her gut. "I can't ignore it anymore. I must listen to it. I have to."

Sometimes our feelings have a message and invaluable insight that we need to listen to. Sometimes we intuitively know what lies beneath our struggles. Sometimes the hardest part is listening to, believing, or trusting that we do, indeed, know something. Lilah's insight during this session was a message for her to live more authentically and truthfully, for her to acknowledge and honor her deep intuition.

I would continue to see Lilah for many years. She would go on to be more and more accepting of her inner knowing. She also began to understand that she had never felt "deserving" of personal time off, of taking mental health days. Because she had been surrounded by working moms, struggling to juggle all their commitments, she didn't feel that her life warranted time off.

Lilah's ability to begin to hone her intuition and honor it allowed her to be more confident in the things that she "just knew," even if she didn't know why. She started sharing her soulful insights with those around her. And while her boss continued to praise her work ethic, her coworkers and clients would tell her how wise and insightful she was. They would tell her how her words guided them, helped them, and reassured them. And as she accepted her deep intuitive gifts more and more, she accepted and honored herself more and more.

In fact, she took a whole summer off one year to regroup, recharge, and refuel.

THE REWARDS OF A FREQUENT FEELER PROGRAM

We have established the importance of having boundaries and tending to our feeling muscle, but if Frequent Feelers thought that was hard, well, here comes the real rub. Because Frequent Feelers experience so much feeling, we need to learn how to stay with and tolerate the hard, difficult, and painful feelings bubbling and churning within us. This may seem unfair at first; after all, there is so much that we already have to navigate.

Sometimes the feelings coming at us feel wonderful, and we welcome them with open arms and an open heart. But many times, they do not feel great. Why would I want to stay with a hard feeling, you might ask? It feels awful, terrible, excruciating. Well, if Frequent Feelers get into the habit of pushing away, numbing, and avoiding yucky feelings, it can become a thing. And by a thing, I mean a habit.

How does it feel to take in...

- Your partner's impatience?
- Your mother's judgment?
- Your friend's frustration?
- Your boss' disappointment?
- Your own despair?

All of the above can generate powerful felt emotion. All of the above can bring forth uncomfortable, even painful felt emotion. If we don't know that we can ride feelings and get past them, we may swallow them. If we don't know we can tolerate and stay with feelings, we may look for a way to numb them or distract ourselves.

Future chapters in this book are devoted to exploring our avoidance of feeling as well as understanding the purpose of our distracting and numbing behaviors. But what is important to grasp right now is that felt emotion can feel so uncomfortable, and, at times, so very painful, that we often look for something else to do other than feeling. And if we habitually do other things and avoid our feelings, we learn and believe, to our detriment, that we can't outlast challenging feelings.

When I finally gained significant insight into my habits of avoidance and numbing feeling – binge eating, retreating from experiences and relationships, holding my breath, tightening muscles throughout my body, shopping, busying myself, and reaching for my phone (emails, texts, news, social media) – I knew I needed to find a way to stay with the feelings I didn't want to feel. Put in simple terms, I needed to stay with, tolerate, and outlast my felt emotion. But boy, was that hard. And I needed some motivation.

So, I created a system of accountability for myself, and there were some rewards built in too. Let's call it... a Frequent Feeler Program. Yes, I earn Frequent Feeler Miles. And over time, I have earned quite a few.

At first, my collection of miles was meager and stark. But every time I sit with a felt emotion, every time I stay with a really challenging feeling, and every time I walk past the refrigerator and let a nagging feeling wax and wane, I earn points. Each time I outlast a tough feeling without scrolling through my emails or doing some online shopping, I get points. Every time I let a feeling wash through me, instead of dumping or discharging the feeling on someone near me, I get points. Now, these points may not get me a free flight to Paris, but they do get me to the other side of a tough feeling – they get me to the other side of a feeling without the need to run as fast as I can in the opposite direction.

Okay, I get it if you're saying to yourself, "Really? All you get for your Frequent Feeler Miles is getting to the other side of a feeling? Hard to see the motivation in that!" One of the questions I get when I tell people about this book is… "Why would I want to sit with a hard feeling? It is such hard work, why do it? There has to be something in it for me." I hear you. I really do. But stay with me and consider these rewards and benefits. When I sit with and get through a challenging feeling without distracting or numbing myself…

- I am more present and awake to myself, my family, and my friends.
- I can take risks, and I am resilient in the face of difficulty because I am not daunted by emotional discomfort.
- I can maintain clean boundaries, and in turn honor my needs, my feeling muscle, and my own voice.

- I have less of a need for numbing and unhealthy behaviors because I can outlast my tough feelings without crutches and distractions.
- I make decisions on how to behave and spend my time with clarity, intention, and self-awareness.
- I take ownership of my feelings rather than discharging the feelings I don't want to feel on the people closest to me.

Who knew I could trade in Frequent Feeler Miles for increased resilience, living in the now with clarity and intention, making healthier choices, and taking responsibility for my feelings? If you're saying, with exuberance (or maybe quiet reluctance), "Sign me up!" then read on.

CHAPTER TWO EXPERIENTIAL

I. BODY PLAY: LET'S SEE WHAT'S BREWING

A common response to the premise of this book is... "I don't know if I feel emotion in my body. It isn't something I've thought about." Fair enough, but let's see.

Let's start by checking in with two places in our body that tend to do a lot of feeling: our chest and our gut. Our chest holds our lungs and our heart, and these organs can generate a lot of feelings. (Remember all the idioms that involve our heart). Our gut can bubble and churn with both small and big feelings. These two areas are a great place to start to feel and sit with emotion. Let's see if anything is brewing.

- **Bring your awareness to your chest:** Find a comfortable position and observe a few inhales and exhales. Notice your ribcage gently expanding and releasing with each breath. As you feel the movement of your breath, go a tad deeper and feel (or imagine) the space that exists in your lungs. Take in the three-dimensionality of your chest and notice how spacious your chest really is. Next, bring your awareness to your heart. Imagine your heart floating in the spaciousness of your chest. Stay here for a few moments. Stay in the roomy expansion of your chest and imagine there is plenty of room for feelings to emerge, spread, and play out. Maybe a feeling is brewing, and maybe not.

- **Bring your awareness to your gut:** Gently move your attention to your gut. If you find yourself caught up in questioning where exactly and anatomically your gut is, let that concern float away. Find your gut by feeling it from the inside. Whatever that means to you. Resist "trying to do it" and mental judgment. Feel the potential space that exists in your gut for feelings to move about. Stay here for a few minutes. Maybe a feeling is brewing, and maybe not.

2. WHERE ARE THESE FEELINGS COMING FROM: A BUBBLE VISUALIZATION

This visualization brings awareness to and helps you manage all the feeling within you and coming at you. It helps you distinguish internal vs. external feelings. You can begin to play with the idea of allowing feelings to move freely within you and around you.

- **Internal feelings** are feelings that arise within you. Examples of internal feelings may be a feeling of heavy eyes when you are tired, a feeling of gnawing hunger before lunch, a wave of desire when your partner walks by, or a tight chest in anticipation of speaking in front of a group.
- Firstly, choose a color that will represent your **internal feelings.** Next, begin to visualize your own feelings encircled in a bubble of the color you chose for internal feelings. Whenever a feeling arises within you, encircle it with a

colored bubble and let it continue to move through you and around you, then allow it to pass and dissipate on its own.

- **External feelings** are feelings that are coming at you from others, not generated within you. Examples are a feeling that your child is hungry and needs you, a feeling that your boss is disappointed in you, a feeling that your mom is waiting impatiently for you, or a feeling that your partner wants your attention.

- Choose a color for **external feelings**. Next, begin to visualize that these external feelings are encircled in a bubble of the color you chose for external feelings. Whenever you feel a feeling coming from outside yourself, encircle it with a colored bubble and let it move around you; if it floats too close to you, gently push it away and allow it to dissipate on its own.

3. JOURNALING EXERCISE

There are a lot of questions posed in this chapter. As you skim back through Chapter Two, consider answering any of the questions that have bullet points. Answering some of these questions will help you discern if you are a Frequent Feeler, how well you take care of and refuel your feeling muscle, and how comfortable you are establishing boundaries. Find a question that piques your interest: meditate on it, write about it, or deeply feel and sit with it.

4. "EMOTIONAL PROFILE" PROMPT

Are you a feeler of emotions? Are you an expressor of emotions? Are you a cognitive processor of emotions? What are all of the ways that these aspects of you intertwine and intermingle within your experience of emotion? You can use my emotional profile (earlier in this chapter) as a model, or not.

Use this statement as a springboard for a journal entry, a painting/picture, a meditation, a poem, a song, a dance, or any form of creative expression.

My emotional profile is...

CHAPTER THREE

THE BODY HOLDS MANY TRUTHS

I constructed tense and rock-like muscles that became my armor – body armor that protected me from so much feeling. The tenser my body got, the less I would feel. I held my breath and tried to be "perfect," so as to avoid making waves in my life; this defense mechanism was an attempt to evade conflict, as conflict was sure to generate difficult or complicated feelings.

I was a dancer for much of my youth and young adulthood. I now see the irony of having spent years dancing, training, and performing. I was drawn to dance and movement because I could not feel my body otherwise. My muscles were so tense and locked, and my breath was so shallow and held, that dance became the only way I could feel my body. Racing across a stage, leaping through the air, and pushing my body beyond its limits were the things that allowed me to feel alive in my body. For me, dance was a way of feeling something.

WHAT IS BODYWORK AND WHAT DOES IT LOOK LIKE?

By now, you have read two of my patients' stories, Frank and Lilah. It's time to take a deeper look at what kind of bodywork I utilize in my practice and what a session on my table looks like.

Bodywork is a very broad term. And if you are fairly new to the term and you were to google the word "bodywork," your head might spin a bit. In fact, the first few definitions that you'll find will actually relate to repairing a car!

After that, you'll find explanations like the following:

- Bodywork is an umbrella term, meaning it encompasses many concepts and techniques.
- Examples of bodywork like massage therapy, chiropractic manipulation, and Reiki may be familiar to you, and yet you may be unacquainted with other elements of bodywork like breathwork, energy medicine, and the mind-body connection.
- Bodywork can have significant effects on both your body and mind; it can improve posture and alignment as well as relieve physical discomfort and emotional stress.
- Bodywork is a bridge to a deeper connection with yourself and can promote self-awareness, mindfulness, and self-discovery.

Because the concept of bodywork is widely unknown and can come across as both vague and sweeping in scope, I thought long and hard about writing this book. How do I present the concept of felt emotion in a relatable and accessible way, when the bodywork lens that I write through is widely untried and untested by many of my readers?

However, there was one thing that I was confident about. I knew that if I could present bodywork through the eyes and experiences of my patients, I could present it in a compelling way. My patients are surely relatable, as their struggles, insights, and stories demonstrate universal struggles, insights, and stories.

When I started to write about my patients' experiences on the table, I was struck by how there were ubiquitous themes intertwined within their complex and unique stories. Life can be so complicated, and yet there are underlying challenges and desires that bleed through. We want fulfillment, connection, and purpose in our lives. We want to feel comfortable and at ease in our bodies and minds. Bodywork is just another way we search for and achieve the things we long for.

So how do I best present the work I do with patients? Well, let's imagine someone is interested in making an appointment with me for bodywork.

How might someone find me? Sometimes, a therapist or psychologist might refer one of their patients to me, especially if the patient is a strong feeler or has somatic complaints that bridge their mental and physical health. At times, individuals have found information about me online or social media and are intrigued. On occasion, a friend has recommended my office. Occasionally, someone makes an appointment after a lecture or class that I give.

What does a session on the table look like? An office visit starts sitting face to face. I always want patients to have the opportunity to check in with me and talk about anything that might have come up during or after our last session. Remember, when we give felt emotion a voice and a vocabulary, it is a fruitful opportunity for patients to articulate and validate their body's inner experience. Additionally, some patients prefer to be quiet for much of the table session, so checking in before and after allows for insights gleaned on the table to have a voice.

When we move from checking in to the bodywork table, patients stay fully clothed. Patients will lie face up, and I place a bolster or a pillow under their knees or head as needed. If they are chilly, I have blankets close by. It is important that patients feel comfortable, warm, and safe because relaxation and a feeling of safety both foster deeper feeling.

As I put my hands on patients, I will often remind them that there are no expectations and no agenda for the session. We are starting from scratch. Whatever a patient is feeling in the moments of our session is what we focus on. Think about it this way – we are practicing being present with ourselves and staying present with what is real for us in any given moment. So, in other words, we work with what we have.

If a patient is anxious, that is where we stay. If a patient is relaxed, that is what we explore. If a patient is rattled or angry or impatient or amused, that is what we work with. The present moment is where the work happens, and being authentic to the present moment means feeling what is real in that moment.

So, your bodywork involves touch. What is that like? Early in my career, the quality of my touch was more forceful and manipulative. What I mean by that is, as a naturopathic physician, I was trained in aspects of chiropractic manipulation, soft tissue manipulation, and massage. And as a result, the bodywork I used early in my practice was focused on correcting misalignment, releasing tension in the body's soft tissues, promoting relaxation, and stress reduction. It's not that my later bodywork was not focused on similar results, but I learned that changes in the body's structure, soft tissue, and energy can happen with a very different kind of touch and intention.

I must credit Craniosacral Therapy for the shift in the quality of my touch. I attended a training workshop in Craniosacral Therapy while still in medical school. This therapy uses a soft touch to assess and enhance the functioning of the craniosacral system – the membranes and cerebrospinal fluid around the brain and spinal cord. I was dumbfounded to learn that this gentle, almost at times imperceptible, touch could make such a seismic shift in the body. I can still remember the workshop leader trying to describe the quality of the touch to the physical therapists and other healthcare professionals attending the training program, as he explained that the touch "listens" to the body.

By incorporating Craniosacral Therapy into my bodywork, my touch completely changed, and while I eventually abandoned Craniosacral Therapy for my "feeling" bodywork, I credit it with helping me trust in a different approach to touch.

My touch is gentle. It is quiet. It listens. It doesn't judge. It does not have expectations or an agenda. It is kind, and it is tolerant. My touch says I can sit with you and stay with you through feelings — pleasant feelings and hard feelings. It says I will keep you and your feelings company, as I am here in this moment with you. And most importantly, my touch is safe and respectful. It does not try to change or manipulate you or your feelings; rather, it honors them.

Having the freedom to dialogue — asking questions as well as identifying, labeling, and giving voice to the bodywork experience — while at the same time using touch as a therapeutic tool is both powerful and an awesome responsibility. When touch and dialogue are combined, it has the potential to be triggering and confusing, as it can blur important therapeutic boundaries. Imagine if an individual has experienced trauma, abuse, or violations involving touch; touch can understandably precipitate difficult, possibly terrifying or paralyzing, feelings. Expectations and boundaries must be established, as it is always my first priority to use touch in a respectful and responsible way. It is of the utmost importance that my patients understand that they have full agency over the process; they can speak up if at any time they are wary of the experience or wish to change direction or stop the session.

How do you describe your work? This may be the hardest question for me to answer. It may be best answered by my decision to write this book. I have struggled mightily to articulate my work and to have the courage to admit and own the work I do. To take ownership of the fact that I am a guide or a shepherd who helps others "to feel" takes a leap of faith. I mean, come on. This is not a real profession, right?

Placing my hands on patients and encouraging them to feel themselves hardly fits into any medical model. Even though naturopathic physicians are trained to treat patients using natural and complementary therapies, we are trained to approach patient care from a diagnosis and treatment model, one that mirrors that of conventional allopathic doctors. Like other physicians, naturopaths create a treatment plan based on clinical and diagnostic findings. But the work I was doing did not fit that mold; in fact, it didn't fit any mold that I was familiar with.

But still, as the years progressed, I leaned in and learned to trust the process. I would follow my patients' lead. We were charting new territory together, and their ability to stay with themselves and articulate their feelings guided me as we went forward. I can't state enough how my patients' commitment to bodywork and their courage to stay with what they were feeling taught me more about the human experience than my years spent studying medicine. I am grateful that they believed in me. I give my patients an enormous amount of credit for taking a chance on me, and for my work growing and thriving with their trust and willingness to feel.

To be honest, it took my stepping away from my practice and taking a sabbatical to be able to truly define my work. The distance from my bodywork table, ironically, allowed me time to reflect on the power of this work. I can now say with confidence, assurance, and commitment that my bodywork table is a place where I hold space for patients to feel their bodies, their feelings, and themselves. The sessions are a time set aside for self-exploration, self-awareness, and feeling. My work allows for an acceptance and a welcoming of deeper feelings – a beginning step for patients to stay with and outlast hard feelings. It has taken me a very long time to own my work and what I do. But it sure feels good to finally do so.

A PERSONAL EXPERIENCE: IT HAD BEEN THERE ALL THE TIME

I was introduced to bodywork in a dance class in college. The class was called Bodies in Motion, and the purpose of acquainting dancers with bodywork was to augment their bodies' intelligence; these techniques allowed dancers to use their bodies in a more efficient way. Like a musician's instrument, the body is the dancer's instrument. Dancers tend to use their bodies in repetitive and strained manners, and when you bring increased awareness to elements that affect your craft – like posture, alignment, and overuse – it can only benefit a dancer's relationship with their instrument.

For me, this introduction to bodywork felt profound. The only way I can put it that would make any sense is that it was as if I was finally speaking to my body in a language that it understood. Suddenly, I felt like everything that I had done with my body up until that point had been imitation or superficial. Bodywork brought me underneath the surface of "my self," so to speak. I felt my body from within for the first time. I am not being overly dramatic when I say that my early experiences with bodywork were transformational.

Imagine having spent almost twenty years of your life in a boat on the surface of the ocean, but you had never felt what water feels like. And one day, for the first time, you dive into the water. The ocean, which had spread in every direction around you for years, was so much more than you had ever imagined. It caressed you, warmed you, and supported you. You felt held by the water in a way you had never been held before. It was as if the water was whispering truths to you as it enveloped you. The water had been there all the time, but you had never touched it.

I was profoundly changed by my first encounters with bodywork. When I was directed to imagine my body melting into the floor and letting the floor support me, I felt grounded. When I was gently guided to release the tension in my jaw, soften my neck and shoulders, and let my pelvis and ribcage widen to support me, I awakened to the potential of ease and comfort in my body, as opposed to effort and pain. When I would place my hands on my belly and breathe gently into my hands, I glimpsed the present moment, perhaps for the first time.

Up until this moment, as both a gymnast and a dancer, I had used my body in ways that had brought results – a high kick, a deep split, a flip with no hands, and the highest leap I could manage. I pushed myself, I hurt myself, and I pushed some more.

Then someone and something said, "Wait!" There's more to it. There is so much more to it. Your body is more than something you just push and force and bend. It speaks. It soars. It rests and recovers. It can be supported and cared for. It doesn't have to work so hard, all the time. And yes, it feels.

BODY BREAK

Take two minutes and... release the tension in your jaw, soften your neck and shoulders, and let your pelvis and ribcage widen to support you. Resist the urge to analyze and to question how to do this the "right way." There is no right way; there is only your way. Quiet your mind and simply let your body respond to the guidance. That's all.

IS BODY ARMOR REALLY A THING?

You will notice that I use the term *body armor* throughout the book. I use this term to refer to the tension we hold in our muscles and soft tissues. These areas can be hard and held, as a result of our recoiling from or pushing away hard feelings. I realize that this may not be a familiar term for some, so let me explain.

Do you ever catch yourself...

- Holding your breath when you are scared or anxious?
- Tensing your jaw, neck, or shoulders when you are worried?
- Gripping your stomach muscles or tightening your chest when you are anticipating failure, shame, rejection, or insecurity?
- Squeezing your fists or tensing your lower back before you speak in front of a group?
- Holding your body in a rigid or guarded posture as you approach a difficult or unfamiliar situation?

If we are anxious and worried a lot of the time, our bodies find themselves in tense and guarded postures a lot of the time. If we perceive the world to be difficult and/or dangerous much of the time, we hold our bodies in rigid and tight postures much of the time. If we hold our breath repeatedly and often, holding our breath becomes a habit, an unconscious pattern.

Bodyworkers have unique insight into this phenomenon of body armor because we see it and feel it in our patients and clients. Tensing, holding, and gripping muscles (as well as other soft tissues) can and does become a habit. We may take for granted the idea that when we are reclining, resting, and sleeping, our muscles automatically release, but this is not the case. Again, bodyworkers will attest to the fact that muscles are held tight even when someone thinks their muscles are relaxed. Tension within the body can become something that we unknowingly and unconsciously maintain throughout our days and nights. This is what I refer to as body armor.

Why the term body armor? Well, one of the purposes of tight and tense muscles is to protect us. Our nervous systems are programmed to respond to stress and danger. Our innate fight or flight response sends us into a protective stance – one that is ready to run from or pounce on a threat at any moment. Not only does our heart rate quicken, and our blood vessels constrict, directing blood to our skeletal muscles, but our shoulders round forward, our head protrudes, and our hamstrings and calves engage. Our bodies instinctually take defensive postures and prepare to engage muscles in times of distress and danger.

When we are worried, anxious, and nervous, our bodies are in distress and feel alarm. This phenomenon is left over from a much earlier time in human evolution. These states of protection, fight, and flight were meant to be momentary as we fought off or fled from predators and perilous situations. These remarkable ways that our bodies protect and guard us from challenges were not meant to be permanent states of being. And yet when we are in a constant or extended period of stress and distress, our bodies adapt and stay guarded.

I have lived with body armor for much of my life, so I know of what I speak. For most of that time, I did not know that my tense body was a reflection of my emotionally guarded inner life. It wasn't until I worked clinically with patients that I began to see similar patterns of holding, guarding, and protecting. I realized that, for many, this held posture of protection had become just a way of life, or rather a way of being. And what was so remarkable and what gave me so much hope was that when my patients began to welcome in feeling, even small amounts of feeling, the tension would start to lessen. I learned through the bravery of my patients that each time we open ourselves to the vulnerability of different feelings within us, we soften just a bit.

THE BREATH IS THE INTERSECTION OF MIND AND BODY

After a medical condition in my mid-twenties resulted in my giving up dancing, I pondered what I should do with my life. For a time, I considered studying bodywork; my exploration of the different forms of bodywork led me to the book *Bone, Breath, & Gesture: Practices of Embodiment,* edited by Don Hanlon Johnson; this book is a collection of writings about and interviews with the pioneers of body-centered therapies. Each chapter describes a different form of bodywork, or "Embodiment." The book opened my mind and my world.

As I read the book, I was drawn to one type of bodywork in particular. It was called "Rosen Method Bodywork." It would be several years before I found myself on the table of a Rosen Method practitioner, but the words of Marion Rosen spoke to me, even then as a very young woman, in a way I could not yet understand. Years after first reading the book, I reread the chapter on the Rosen Method and found these words highlighted by my younger self:

"Naturally, as we come into this world, we are not beings that hold back; we are beings that are open... But we put something in the body that makes it more difficult to move, and we freeze in this position. Why does this happen? There is always something that seems to necessitate a certain way of non-movement, non-living in a certain way. And every time something stimulates it again, we hold again. We hold a little bit more. And we have forgotten that this is what we do. These elements are partly in the physical body and partly in our emotional being."

Marion Rosen, from *Rosen Method: An Approach to Wholeness and Well-Being Through the Body* by Elaine L. Mayland, Ph.D.

In my early years as a naturopathic physician, I found myself part of a small group of Rosen Method students and practitioners. The first thing that I needed to understand about the work was the importance of the diaphragm, the largest of the muscles responsible for breathing. The diaphragm is not something we talk much about in medical school or in healthcare in general, so it took some time to wrap my head around this focus on our breath and one of the muscles responsible for it.

The diaphragm is a muscle that sits between the chest and the abdomen, as it attaches to the sternum, spine, and lower rib cage; it is one of the primary muscles that we use to breathe. Because the diaphragm is under both voluntary and involuntary control, it is a rather unique muscle in the body. Breathing is involuntary, as it happens without our control, but we can also voluntarily affect or change how we breathe. As a result, breathing is linked to both our conscious and unconscious selves. This link makes it important, and Rosen believed that it is a place to find distinctive insight.

Through her work with clients, Rosen found that when the diaphragm is held and tight, the body does not function efficiently and with ease. She also noticed something remarkable — muscles of the body, including the diaphragm and, consequently, the breath, will soften and release when emotion surfaces. Her work with clients demonstrated that when our bodies and our diaphragms are tense and restricted, we stay at a distance, so to speak, from ourselves and our emotions.

I attended Rosen Method retreats and workshops led by Susan Brenner. Brenner and Rosen coauthored *Rosen Method Bodywork: Accessing the Unconscious through Touch*. During the workshops that I attended, Brenner offered us opportunities to glean insight into the diaphragm, as we would take turns working with each other on a table as "practitioner" and "client." When we were the client, lying on the table, we would experience firsthand how feeling emotion or stumbling across a realization — like I'm holding my breath, I'm feeling fear, I'm hard on myself, I'm gripping my jaw — would be accompanied by a softening of the diaphragm, a slightly easier, softer, or deeper breath, that was perceptible to both the practitioner and the client.

What fascinated me to no end was that our breath would change when our bodies were touched deeply by an emotional experience or some kind of truth about ourselves. I was spellbound by the idea that the body had an inner knowing — a knowing when we would touch something authentic or genuine within ourselves. A connection, an emotion, an insight, a truth.

The idea that when we feel a part of ourselves that we have avoided or numbed, we soften and release would go on to influence my work with patients in a profound way. I fully embraced Rosen's insight that our willingness and courage to feel more of ourselves would result in a softening and a releasing of our protective armor. And as the years progressed and I forged my own work with patients, I would see again and again how a tight, held muscle is often numb to sensation, and yet conversely, a released, softened muscle awakens to increased sensation. Ultimately, thanks to Rosen Method Bodywork, I made a far-reaching and remarkable connection that would stand as the foundation for pursuing and continuing my feeling work — when we feel, we touch a truth.

KIRK: IT IS THE TRUTH, MY TRUTH

Kirk came to me for help after a recent diagnosis of irritable bowel syndrome (IBS). Kirk was a bit of a conundrum to me because I couldn't get a clear picture of his health history or his personal history. He would tell me different things on different visits that didn't align. I was able to discern that he was a musician, and to supplement his income, he taught young children and adults to play various instruments. He was married, and his house was full of dogs that he and his husband had adopted.

I got to know Kirk over the course of a six- or seven-year time span
and roughly three to four dozen office visits. Each time he came to
me, he would fill me in on his life – how his dogs were doing and
the trips he and his husband would take around the world. As he
would talk, I remember feeling as if he were wearing a mask. His eyes
were somewhat blank, and his face had minimal expression. I had a
hard time following his stories as they were not always linear, and he
jumped from topic to topic.

Kirk had come to me for nutritional guidance specifically around his
IBS, but he was interested in bodywork as well. He had read on my
website that I believe our bodies have a story to tell (this was how
I originally described my bodywork), and that comment resonated
with him. During his first session, Kirk was very quiet on the table.
He responded very little to the few questions I asked. His body was
quiet too, and his breath was so still. His inhales were small, almost
imperceptible, and there was noticeable tension in all the muscles of
his chest and abdomen.

I remember noting to myself that I didn't feel much under my hands.
I had a hard time feeling him as I touched him. While this comment
might seem unusual, bodyworkers will know what I mean. Sometimes
bodies can have very little energy and vitality within them, and they
emanate a certain blankness or absence. Kirk's body felt both blank
and very tense.

I talked him through a guided meditation to bring some softening to
his held body. When he got off the table, I got the impression he was

unimpressed by the experience. He came back a handful of times for bodywork over the course of about a year, and then I did not hear from him for a while.

After an absence of roughly three years, Kirk returned to my office. His demeanor struck me as very different. His eyes were brighter, and he was looking at me with more intention and clarity. He spoke to me in a more direct manner. "I wasn't completely honest with you when I was here last," he said. "I have been seeing a therapist for over two years now. I am in a twelve-step program right now. I have a sponsor."

Kirk explained with remarkable clarity how he had started to see a therapist and, with his therapist's help, had admitted to himself that he was an alcoholic. He had been attending A.A. meetings for almost two years. His husband was both proud and supportive of him, and he was attending ALANON meetings as well.

Kirk reminded me of the comment on my website that had initially piqued his interest in my work. "Our bodies have a story," he reminded me. Kirk said with great intention, "I want to start weekly bodywork sessions."

I told Kirk that I wanted to make sure he was in a strong and supported place to explore his body's story. I told him that I had initially had a hard time following his backstory, and I wanted to know more about him before jumping back into bodywork. We spent that visit taking a thorough health history, both physical and mental, and Kirk's clarity and candor were quite impressive.

On his next visit, we went right to the table. When I put my hands on him, he was buzzing with a lot of energy. He told me he was excited. After about ten minutes, I felt a shift in his energy. It went from loudly buzzing to gently humming.

Kirk told me that he was seeing a lot of "purple" behind his eyes and some "red" in his belly. I put one hand on his belly and one hand on his diaphragm. "Can you stay with the colors you are seeing?" I asked.

It is not uncommon for patients to see colors within their bodies during a bodywork session. Some patients might see words or hear music. Some may see or feel images or memories. It is important to the work that patients feel comfortable and never judged, so they feel free to accurately describe what comes up for them.

Kirk continued, "Yes, the purple is vibrant, and it is swirling. The red is very still and heavy. The colors are very real. They are both inside me."

I stayed quietly with Kirk, my hands remained on his diaphragm and abdomen. Suddenly, I felt Kirk take a soft but deep breath. The inhale and exhale felt significant and distinct. The breath was soft and easy, but deep and noticeable at the same time. I asked him if he had noticed the breath.

Yes, he said immediately. "The colors make sense now," he said. "The purple is my hope, my light. The red is my fear. I'm so scared I will start drinking again." He took another deep breath. "I'm so proud of myself, but my sobriety feels fragile."

I waited a few minutes. "Kirk, that is such an honest and vulnerable thing to feel and to say out loud," I said.

"Yes," Kirk said, "but it is the truth, my truth."

OUR FELT EMOTION IS A TRUTH

In the next chapter we will take a deeper look at how our thoughts do not always have our back. What I mean by that is the soundtrack that plays through our mind day after day often contains thoughts and beliefs that are simply not true. Of course, we tell ourselves things and believe things about ourselves that are helpful, constructive, and accurate. But the point I am trying to make is that we can be, at times, deceived by our own thoughts.

Consider a critical thought you might have about yourself, like "I'm not interesting to others;" this is probably not true. It is distinctively possible that a narrative you tell yourself about a current situation, like "My coworkers are thinking that I don't know what I am doing right now," is exaggerated, misguided, or patently false. If you are someone who believes that "I will always fail at the important things in my life," you are listening to an inner voice that is not helpful and not accurate, despite all the evidence you think you may have to the contrary.

While our thoughts and beliefs can be deceptive at times, our bodies, our inner experience, and our felt emotion authentically reflect our present moment. Our felt emotion is true for us in the moment, even if our words and thoughts are not. For example, we may perceive a situation to be dangerous and unsafe; whether or not this is an accurate perception, our felt emotion of danger is real to us. The heavy feeling of fear that resides in our gut in that moment is real and true. I may be completely off base during a party, and say to myself, "The friends I am with right now don't want me here with them," but the rejection that I feel in my body is true to me in that moment. You might be 100% right that your boss is disappointed in you today, and your felt emotion of inadequacy mirrors that perception accurately.

Whether a feeling is appropriate to the situation or not, the felt emotion is an inner truth. I remember well an encounter with Ava, a fellow dancer, many years back. She came into the dance studio changing room and immediately looked in the mirror. "Wow," she said. "I've been feeling gross all day because I thought I looked terrible. But I don't look half bad," she said with a chuckle. That moment has stayed with me because it was such a clear example of how someone's day can be ruled by a false narrative.

As dancers we look in the mirror for a lot of the day. The mirror can become a reflection of our insecurities and our critical view of self. There is very little objective reality going on when our perceived imperfections and negative self-image are all we see. Personally, I thought Ava looked gorgeous that day; in fact, she always looked gorgeous to me. My mind was blown that such a beautiful young woman had insecurities, just like me.

Sadly, Ava's feeling "gross" all day was her truth all day. She felt it, lived it, and embodied it. It didn't matter that everyone who saw her that day most likely agreed with my view of Ava; instead, she was stuck in her "gross" truth. When her truth changed as she looked in the mirror and took in her fabulousness, I saw Ava's whole demeanor change. She stood taller and more confident. She took up more space in the room and had a wide smile, as her felt experience of herself shifted from "gross" to "not half bad."

Remember that our felt emotion is an important inner data point. It is data that our bodies communicate to us in real time. As you continue through the pages of this book, you will notice how powerful it is to stay with and honor a feeling — yours or someone else's. Of course, we don't have the time to honor all the feelings we have, nor should we; we'd never get anything done! But because we live in such a busy world, feelings are rarely noticed or acknowledged, and thus we neglect and gloss over this important data — these little gems of truth that are generated within us throughout our day.

If we can carve out a little space, no matter how brief or how small, and check in with an occasional feeling, we may notice things that are worth noticing. We may notice that, like Ava, we walk around feeling bad about ourselves for much of the day, and we don't need to. Or we may notice, like Kirk did, that we are proud of ourselves for a major accomplishment but also frightened that it could slip away. We may find that, like Lilah in Chapter Two, we don't feel deserving of something, like time off, that we so desperately need to thrive and be well.

Can we find even a small amount of space in life for feeling and felt emotion? If we could, we would see that the data we glean from our feeling muscle is valid and worth collecting. We would notice that the data we are glossing over is, at times, of great significance. Because when a truth comes our way that has some insight or wisdom attached, we want to know about it.

CHAPTER THREE EXPERIENTIAL

I. BODY PLAY: LET'S SEE WHAT LIES BENEATH THE SURFACE

The idea of body armor suggests two things: we have a hard surface and a softer inside. Let's play with these two ideas.

First, we must address two common misconceptions. Some folks put up a barrier to "softening the body" because they equate it with "not being in shape." And at the same time, some people celebrate "hard bodies," as it equates to being muscular and fit. For this BODY PLAY, we need to throw both those ideas out the window.

In this visualization, "Hardening" is the tension we create in our bodies to push away vulnerability and to build walls of protection; feeling the tension in the body is the opening to exist differently within ourselves. "Softening" is where we embrace feeling vulnerable, and our bodies melt into the support, acceptance, and safety of self-awareness.

- **Can you feel the tension:** Find a comfortable position and begin to slowly scan your body (this is a scan of inner sensations) from head to toe. Are there areas of your body that are numb? Are there areas of discomfort? Are there areas where your muscles are held tight? Resist trying too hard to find tension in your body; instead, let your body guide you and speak to you. Play with the idea of listening to your body. Your body will tell you where you are held and tense.

- **Embrace softening:** Once you have identified an area in your body that is held, tense, or guarded, stay with that area. Gently observe that area. Avoid trying to change or "do" something. Take a moment and acknowledge what supports you. If you are sitting, your support is the chair. If you are lying down or standing, your support is the floor. You can extend the concept of support to people in your lives, your safety net, your livelihood, your passions, commitments, and spiritual pursuits. Once you have found your support, then allow your tension to melt or soften into what supports you. Try not to get caught up in questioning how to do it "the right way." Let your body show you the way.

2. BREATH AWARENESS

Breath awareness is any type of exercise that brings your attention to your breathing. You can engage in a breath awareness practice at any time and in any place. The MOST IMPORTANT aspect of breath awareness is to resist the urge to change or manipulate your breath in any way; there is no right or wrong way to breathe in this exercise – leave judgment and agenda at the door. There are a lot of breathing techniques that direct, guide, or dictate how you breathe; this awareness exercise is NOT asking you to do anything with your breath other than simply notice each inhale and exhale.

Find a quiet time of day when you have a few moments to yourself. Find a comfortable position and bring your attention to your inhale and exhale. It may be helpful to place a hand on your belly, diaphragm, or sternum so that you can feel the inhale and exhale. Simply observe your breath for approximately five minutes. That's all.

Once you have tried this in a quiet place, you can bring awareness to your breath for a few minutes while you are going about other activities, like washing the dishes, watering the plants, taking a walk, or talking with a friend.

3. "SOMETHING I TELL MYSELF THAT IS NOT TRUE" PROMPT

Use this statement as a springboard for a journal entry, a painting/picture, a meditation, a poem, a song, a dance, or any form of creative expression.

A thought, belief, or narrative that I know is NOT true, but I tell myself anyway is...

CHAPTER FOUR

THINKING VS. FEELING

At different times in my life, I found myself in therapy talking about and analyzing my feelings yet still avoiding feeling them. The discomfort I felt in my body – the heartaches, the loneliness, the inadequacy, the shame, the fear – sent me to my head and my thoughts. Because the felt emotion of my loneliness, shame, and fear was simply too much for me to bear, I retreated to my mind. I excelled in all my years of schooling; I tried so hard to be perfect. But my mind was so very busy – worrying, ruminating, and obsessing. As my thoughts cycled in rapid succession, it felt as if my head would explode.

WE ARE MORE THAN OUR THOUGHTS

If we consider our Western society's emphasis on thinking and intellect, we can understand why we are less likely to prioritize feeling our emotions over other more "heady" endeavors. Emotion is often portrayed as primal and irrational – an aspect of our animal instinct – while our cerebral enterprises are celebrated and highly esteemed. When we have been overtaken by emotion, we can no longer be counted on to be clear- or levelheaded.

In a world and a culture that place great value on the pursuits of the mind – intellect, creativity, and innovation – the physical body gets mostly relegated to sports and recreation. And emotions are pretty much confined to the therapist's couch, the warm arms of a caregiver, parent, or partner, or maybe the wisdom of a teacher or spiritual advisor.

Consider for a moment how much emphasis and value our Western culture places on thinking. From early on in grade school all the way to high school, the majority of our days are spent at a desk or table exercising our brains. Math, language arts, science, and social studies dominate the curriculum and the hours our children spend at school. With the exception of alternative forms of schooling, the structure of our children's day reveals that learning, academics, and time sitting in class completely outweigh time spent on other endeavors.

If we are lucky, our physical body will be exercised a bit too. Physical education makes up one period in the school day, often only every other day. Recess time is simultaneously being cut back as the academic requirements and expectations of our children continue to balloon. Yes, sports can be a significant and meaningful part of a child's life, but at times, we see competitiveness and winning take precedence over the emotional benefits of physical activity and team collaboration.

The emotional health of a child is, for sure, gaining more importance in the larger consciousness of our school system. School administrators, counselors, and teachers understand and care about children's emotional health; some care very deeply indeed, but in the vast majority of schools, it continues to be placed at a lower priority than academic and intellectual study. And this reinforces the overarching message that emotional health is, at best, less important.

Mathematics and grammar exercise our thinking muscles, and likewise gym class exercises our skeletal muscles. Feeling our emotions – guilt, jealousy, empathy, delight – exercises our feeling muscle. Our feeling muscle needs to be nurtured and tended to, and if from an early age, we prioritize our ability to feel, label, and talk about emotions, we foster and nurture our emotional intelligence.

We know intuitively that tending to the emotional health of our children and ourselves has benefits. Doesn't it seem sensible and plausible to explore a more equal sharing of our resources between the emotional and intellectual parts of us? Chances are "thinking" will continue to take precedent over "feeling" in our society, but maybe we can make a small (or perhaps big) shift toward balance in the way we "think" about "feeling."

OUR COGNITIVE EXPERIENCE OF EMOTION

Our intellectual or analytical experience of emotion is something that happens as we grow and develop. As our consciousness of ourselves grows and our cognitive and intellectual ability develops, we can think about our emotions rather than just feel them. Take babies and toddlers for example; we know that emotion is felt and expressed without, or with very little, thought getting in the way. Toddlers do emotion so well; they feel freely and loudly and often. My son did frustration and impatience so well as a toddler that he would have won a gold medal, if tantruming were an Olympic sport. As we grow and learn, however, we begin to filter our emotions through a mental construct.

Throughout grade school we adjust our emotional reactions based on our early understanding of societal rules and expectations. If Henry throws my toy truck over the playground fence, I can begin to think, reason, and understand what an appropriate reaction is. I may realize that screaming at him or hitting him is not appropriate playground behavior, even if that's exactly what I want to do. Instead, I can use my words to tell Henry that I'm frustrated and that it is not fair that he did not respect my property. I can make a cognitive choice to respond in a socially acceptable manner. Indeed, it is imperative that we develop and hone this ability to understand our emotions and be able to manage them and then react and respond accordingly.

Additionally, the ability to talk about how we are feeling is crucial to our emotional health. There exists a robust understanding and acknowledgment in mental health that sharing and talking about feelings has a multitude of benefits. Being able to name and label feelings helps validate them. We realize we are not alone or unique in our feelings, when we see or hear others living through similar emotions. We feel heard, understood, and supported when we share our feelings. Talking about feelings takes the pressure out of the pressure cooker of feelings; emotions don't get pent up or stuffed down. When we give voice to our feelings, we liberate them. We set them free.

To put it succinctly, a cognitive and analytical understanding of emotion allows us to manage and control our emotions so that we act and behave appropriately. As we mature, we know what is expected of us from the classroom to the boardroom. From our family of origin and childhood experiences, we have a sense of where it is acceptable to feel and express emotion and where it is not. Based on the comfort level of our caregivers, friends, and family, we will have a good idea of whom we can talk about our feelings with, who will meet and greet those conversations with support and a listening, caring ear, and who will not.

While the crux of this book is to explore and assert that the body is our feeling muscle, I am not diminishing the importance of our cognition. In fact, if I may lean on Goleman's *Emotional Intelligence* once again, he lays out the concept of Emotional

Literacy, and the power it holds for our children. Emotional Literacy is the development of self-awareness around naming emotions and identifying their causes, as well as the understanding, managing, and controlling of emotional behaviors, and it is paramount for a healthy and successful life. Being able to read emotions in others and thus have success in our personal and professional relationships is a powerful argument for continuing our emotional education throughout our lifetimes.

I humbly build on the concept of emotional intelligence by highlighting the body's contribution to it — essentially giving the body some well-earned credit. While I am attempting to make the case for felt emotion to have a rightful place on the emotional map, I am not underestimating or diminishing the significance that an analytical and intellectual understanding of emotion has on our human experience. It is essential to our self-awareness, our ability to reflect, and our ability to live a successful and meaningful life.

JULIAN: I REALLY DO HAVE A BODY AFTER ALL

Julian called my office and had a lot of questions for me. What is a naturopathic physician? What is your training? What would a visit with you look like? How much would it cost? How long will I be there? How many visits will I need until I'm better?

I could confidently answer all of his questions except the last one. When I get the question, "How many visits will I need until I'm better?" (and Julian was not the first to ask the question), I know immediately that this particular patient does not view working with me as a process. He is hoping to be cured within a finite and predictable timeline. And I understand that. I really do.

I explained to Julian that my practice follows a mind-body medicine model and that my work is more process-oriented. I offered to refer him to one of the many excellent naturopaths in the area who practice primary family care.

"No," he said abruptly. A friend had recommended my office, and he wanted to see me, even if I could not guarantee a precise timeframe or an expected duration of our work together.

On his first visit, Julian told me, in a rapid-fire manner, his list of concerns. Tension headaches, reflux, and occasional insomnia. "How can you help?" he asked pointedly and somewhat impatiently after he had given me his chief complaints and his medical history.

For much of that session, I wore my naturopathic physician hat, instead of my bodyworker hat, and wrote down on my prescription pad some nutritional, herbal, and lifestyle recommendations for him. He seemed momentarily appeased.

I mentioned the possibility of doing some bodywork, perhaps some relaxation techniques that he could use at home. He looked at me with great suspicion and what I could only surmise was a combination of both doubt and agitation. But after all, his friend had recommended me, so he would give it a try.

Not only did he give it a try, but he came back again. The supplements I had recommended had helped with his various complaints, and he was surprised at how much he enjoyed the relaxation and bodywork. He was impressed (and frankly convinced) that the breathing exercises I gave him as homework had eased his reflux.

On our fourth session, we went directly to the table after a brief check-in. He was on the table for only a few minutes when he noticed a strong tightness that he said was gripping his lower chest. I placed my hands at the base of his lower ribcage and encouraged him to stay with the feeling. He stayed with this gripping tightness for a good ten minutes. Under my hands, I felt his muscles beginning to soften as he brought breath into the area under my hands. I noticed a few very deep inhales. His exhales also became easier – less forced and less effortful – and slightly elongated.

He remained very quiet for most of the session, and I stayed with him, my hands softly on the intersection of his ribcage and abdomen. "I really haven't felt my body in a long time. I mean really felt it. You know what I mean," he said as the session came to a close. I quietly nodded in agreement.

Julian continued, "I think I have been a talking head for a long time now, only feeling myself from the neck up. I really do have a body after all, don't I?" Julian had a softer look and briefly smiled at his insight.

Julian's predicament is far from unique. His revelation about it, however, is both rare and remarkable. Many of us are walking around as talking heads, to some extent or a great extent, without the awareness of our mind-body disconnect. I am not making a cynical or derogatory statement when I note that someone walks around as a talking head; it is simply a result of the increased and ever-present emphasis we place on our minds and intellect – and all the remarkable innovation and creation that comes of it. For some of us, our bodies are mere appendages to the highly esteemed and more distinguished head and brain. When we connect the two, body and mind, we are simply more whole and holistic – a more complete human.

It was such a relief for Julian to have that insight. He smiled to himself as he got off the table, and seemed less burdened and more integrated (head, neck, and body) as he left my office.

Julian would come back to my office, off and on over the next five years, for the occasional ailment. I would put on my naturopathic hat and write down some recommendations, and after about ten minutes, he would ask, "When are we going to the table?"

MESSAGES CAN GET IN THE WAY OF FEELING

As we grow up, our inner self takes in many messages from the outside world. These messages are a way where our "thinking," and quite frankly the thinking of others, can muddle and hijack our ability to feel. These outside messages can come in the form of societal pressures and norms as well as the media. Messages also come from those closest to us, like family, teachers, coaches, and other caregivers.

These messages implant and imprint on our consciousness. Some of these messages are helpful, and some are not.

There are many terrific books today geared toward young people that give children permission to feel all their feelings – both the feelings that feel really great and even the ones that don't. These books give kids words to describe their feelings and a vocabulary that validates strong emotion. Books with thoughtful messages around emotional intelligence nurture our feeling muscle as well as a general openness to accept feelings without judgment.

One of my absolute favorite books, which I read over and over to my children when they were little, is Jamie Lee Curtis's *Today I Feel Silly & Other Moods that Make My Day*. Curtis beautifully presents feelings as everyday occurrences and delivers, in a charming and candid way, an important message to young people – no matter the feeling, be it cranky, joyful, lonely, or silly, it's all okay. As a Frequent Feeler myself, I couldn't think of a better message for my children, as apples do not fall far from the tree.

With the help of children's books like Curtis's and movies like *Inside Out 2*, when we present our emotions as commonplace and familiar concepts, we demystify feelings that feel hard or yucky.

So, my grumpiness is visiting me a little bit this morning.
No biggie. Feeling grumpy is normal and okay. I know it will pass.

Chances are that if you're reading this book, you may have grown up before these kinds of books were widely accessible. And even if you have had the great fortune to come across these books and/or similar messages in your childhood, those messages may not have always been reinforced by caregivers, teachers, and others in your life.

Without reinforcement, even the best book and the most well-intentioned message can only plant the seed. We need positive modeling and guidance, and someone willing to hold a nonjudgmental space for our feelings. To grasp and embody these concepts, we must grow up in a very different world than the one most of us grew up in.

The fast-paced and goal-oriented society that exists today can't help but find feelings, particularly the uncomfortable ones, both inconvenient and intolerable. And when there are people to see, places to be, and things to do, feelings just get in the way of getting stuff done.

From an early age, we get the message that feelings, especially ones like anger and sadness, are just plain inconvenient — not to be felt in public and sometimes not at home either. We internalize these messages. Our anger is met with "This is not the time or place for that!" Our tears are met with "Boys don't cry" or "Hold it together." Our fears might be belittled or ridiculed. Our loneliness and rejection may trigger our caregivers' own similar feelings of loneliness and rejection — feelings that they don't want to feel in themselves, let alone tolerate in us.

In response to these messages, we begin to swallow our shame, stuff our humiliation, and sit on our anger. When we learn not to express emotion, we learn to hide our feelings from others and in turn hide them from ourselves as well. Remember that our cognitive ability to analyze, judge, and manage our emotions is helpful in ensuring that we comply with societal norms and expectations; this is vital for our successful integration into the world around us. But our cognitive ability to analyze, judge, and manage our emotions also gets in the way of our comfort, ease, and ability to stay with hard feelings.

What if we questioned the message of "This is not the time or place for that" with a response, like

- Well, when is the time for that feeling?
- Where is the appropriate place to feel?
- If not in public, where? If not in the cereal aisle of the grocery store, then where?
- If not during Dad's important phone call, then when?
- If not with frustration and at the top of my lungs, then how?

Even the best-intentioned caregiver doesn't always have the right answers, the best answers, or even helpful answers. Being the parent of a daughter and a son, who both had no trouble expressing their anger, fear, sadness, and disgust, both at home and in full display in restaurants and grocery stores, I sympathize. And I know all too well the frustration and the knee-jerk reaction to get them to stop.

Certain emotions and behaviors are triggering to us as parents. Sometimes, caregivers have unintentionally passed on their own intolerance of emotions. And sometimes, a caregiver has shut down an emotion that threatened to cause a scene or public stir. As children, we heed these messages. For example, a tantrum in the grocery store line is simply unacceptable; our immediate response is often to quell the outbreak or outburst of emotion as quickly as we possibly can.

I can remember shutting down (or at least trying to) my son's temper tantrums in the grocery store with words like "Stop it right now" or the dreaded "What will people think?" Yes, I used shame and my own embarrassment as excuses for him to calm down. In my stressed-out mom's brain, there wasn't time, space, or room for emotion. It was embarrassing, annoying, and enraging that my son would resist being strapped into the grocery cart. I mean, his audacity! When what I really needed was for him to be calm and acquiescent.

Our children's inherent need – to both feel what they are feeling as well as to express what they are feeling – becomes inconvenient in such a fast-moving family. Temper tantrums in the grocery aisles, tears and frustration getting into car seats or putting on bulky winter clothing, fears and need for reassurance around going to bed, and anxiety being dropped off at daycare or school – all of these feelings taken separately and at face value seem like just another part of growing up, just a part of being a small human. But all of these scenarios, combined with having to be in two places at once and running ten minutes behind and needing to fill up the gas tank and having your boss breathing down your neck, mean there is no time for this feeling nonsense.

When my kids were little, I remember having a discussion with a mom's group that I was a part of. One of the moms was so insightful when she realized that her children's powerful emotions were not only super inconvenient for her in the moment, but they were also hugely triggering for her. A public display of any kind of difficult emotion brought up how her own parents had reacted to her anger and even how they had felt when she expressed other emotions. I found her awareness so compelling because we do intuitively feel our parents' discomfort. We do instinctively know when our parents are frustrated or embarrassed or enraged. As children, we register our caregivers' discomfort, we take it in, and we embody it.

When I think back to my own upbringing, the concept of nature vs. nurture is clearly at play. I'm sure that my parents could have tended to my emotional health in ways that would have better benefited the Frequent Feeler within me, but, for sure, they did the very best they could. My parents were so well-intentioned and thoughtful in how they cared for and nurtured me; the reality was that there was no roadmap for raising a child who felt so much and so strongly. Notwithstanding my great fortune of being blessed with immensely kind and loving parents, I still struggled with my own emotional discomfort and ended up shutting down and numbing my felt emotion. I was born a Frequent Feeler, and without tools to manage all the feeling, I was overwhelmed a lot of the time. Despite what our little people think about adults, parents don't always have all the answers. We simply do the best we can.

Whether our caregivers are well-intentioned, oblivious, or overwhelmed themselves, the way they manage and understand their own emotions can dictate how we manage and understand our own emotions — how free or restrained we are in our expression of emotion, how we react to others expressing emotions, and how available we are to actually stay with our own feelings of strong emotion. The way we are raised can embed within us, if we're lucky, a general sense of comfort with emotion or, if not, the possibility of being wary of emotions and feeling in general.

In some cases, a strong distrust of emotions can be passed down from generation to generation. When our displays or outbursts of emotion are deemed unacceptable or inconvenient, we may get the message that feeling any emotion is insufferable and intolerable as well. Our feeling muscle gets the message that emotions are not to be expressed and not to be discussed and that can easily translate to the message that emotions shouldn't be felt either. Combine the fact that strong emotion can be painful to feel with the messages about feeling that abound in our society, and the overwhelming implication may be "Stay far, far away from that perilous stuff called feeling."

BODY BREAK

Set the book aside for a few minutes and... take a moment to feel your neck. Embrace an awareness that your neck connects your head to the rest of your body. Allow your neck to soften. Allow your throat to soften. Resist the urge to "try to figure out" how to soften your neck and throat. Simply let the words translate to an inner body experience. Soften your neck and throat. That's all.

YOUR INNER CRITIC VS. YOUR NEUTRAL OBSERVER

Another place where our thinking vs. feeling can get all tangled up is when our inner critical voice wakes up and gets loud. Say hello to your Inner Critic. Your Inner Critic is a close friend and confidant who visits you frequently. This familiar inner voice loves to comment, judge, and critique the human experience. Your Inner Critic can take over any or all of your emotional experiences and can shut down your feeling or your expression of emotion with ease and lightning speed. Sometimes the Inner Critic teams up with shame, embarrassment, and doubt, and hijacks the whole shebang, shutting emotion down altogether.

Does a voice in your head ever tell you that...

- You shouldn't feel or show "negative" emotions? Anger is ugly and unacceptable?
- You shouldn't tell anyone you are sad or lonely? Crying shows weakness?
- You should hide your frustration? Be strong and hold it all in?
- You are a bad person if you feel jealous? Apathetic? Insecure?

Our Inner Critic is a mental construct that wraps up all our experiences, knowledge, and messages and creates beliefs about our behaviors, thoughts, and actions. It manifests as a voice that lives within us, in our head, or over our shoulder, and comments often and freely. Remember my dancer friend Ava, whose Inner Critic was hard at work. Our Inner Critic is amazingly loud and confident in its critical examination of who we are and what we do. And it is adept at catching us off guard with a pointed comment that can derail any situation.

It is important that we get to know and recognize our Inner Critic. This self-awareness – starting to notice when your Inner Critic rears its head – is part of a mindfulness practice that we can begin to embrace at any time (see the experiential section at the end of the chapter). As we begin to notice how often our Inner Critic visits us throughout a given day and how well developed and thriving it is within us, it will be reassuring to learn that we have a built-in antidote to this loud and quite assertive Inner Critic.

Meet your Neutral Observer, perhaps a much less familiar player. Your Neutral Observer is an important player to counteract your Inner Critic, and as you will come to find, plays an important role in feeling your emotions too. Your Neutral Observer is a gentle, nonjudgmental presence within you. This neutral presence takes time and insight to develop, while the Inner Critic just grows like a well-watered and overfed weed. Your Inner Critic is nourished by the messages you take in, the outer voices you hear, and your own insecurities and doubt, whereas cultivating your Neutral Observer entails embracing and learning a whole new way to approach your inner life.

The Neutral Observer is a more productive and more constructive player within our self-awareness. The mindless chatter, the rumination, and the endless worry of our Inner Critic can take us in circles, and the critiquing and judging of our experience can turn us upside down. Conversely, the Neutral Observer simply notices our mental soundtrack, and it detaches from the words and narratives we use to describe our experiences. By nurturing and growing a gentle acceptance and a nonjudgmental attitude, we can actually stop the Inner Critic in its tracks. The Neutral Observer takes more energy and commitment to develop, but in the end, the Inner Critic is no match for a grounded and unflappable Neutral Observer.

My Inner Critic: As regret sets in, she goes up into my head and cues the narrative of the many missed opportunities and all the risks I never took. She tells me that I didn't open that one door that would have changed my life for the better. She notices the twisting and heaviness in my chest, and she just chalks the feeling off as another bothersome, annoying, and useless feeling to ignore. My Inner Critic tells me that I have wasted time in my life and that I will never get that time back.

My Neutral Observer: As she senses a wave of regret swelling within me, she simply observes the twisting sensation behind my sternum and notices a coating around my heart that is heavy and cold. She stays with the feeling until the twisting loosens and the heavy coating starts to melt away. My Neutral Observer notices that sometimes I attach words of blame to the regret that I am feeling, but she remains detached from the narrative and simply observes.

If I'm being completely honest, I have found the Neutral Observer to be frustratingly fleeting. Boy, is that Inner Critic ever-present and tenacious. It does indeed take persistent dedication to develop and nurture a neutral eye, but I assure you the pursuit is worthwhile and rewarding. For most of us living a busy, fast-paced life, our Neutral Observer has been deprived of oxygen, while in contrast, our critical voice has thrived in a rushed and ungrounded environment full of opportunities to critique and naysay.

Fostering your Neutral Observer has a long list of side effects – including acceptance, gentleness, compassion, and kindness toward yourself. Now, those are side effects I can get behind! You will meet both your Inner Critic and your Neutral Observer as you read on. Keep them in mind, as they are important to get acquainted with.

BETH: HER LIFELONG INNER CRITIC

Beth was a professor who had recently been diagnosed with ovarian cancer. She had been divorced for many years and lived by herself. A thoughtful and insightful woman, she had been reading two different books simultaneously, both on the mind-body connection, and wanted to prepare her "mindset," as she put it, for the months of treatment ahead.

Beth believed that if she approached her cancer diagnosis and treatment with a more "positive" outlook, then her outcome would be better. It is not uncommon for patients recently diagnosed with cancer to make an appointment with me. A cancer diagnosis can be both terrifying and disorienting and can compel individuals to take a deep look at their lives.

Beth wasn't really sure she wanted to do bodywork; rather, she wanted to discuss a few connections and insights she had made while reading one of her books. She repeated to me that she was concerned that her "negative" and fearful thinking was not helpful while undergoing treatment.

During her first session, we discussed what she meant by "negative" thinking. She revealed to me that she had had, for as long as she could remember, a very negative voice that filled her mind throughout the day. I asked her to give me some examples of her thoughts. "You're overweight. You're not attractive or interesting to people. Stop talking, no one cares. If only you were smarter or had more interesting things to say, you would have gained more respect from your students and colleagues," Beth listed these examples quickly and confidently. Beth did not have to try hard to find her critical voice; rather, it was on top of mind and at the tip of her tongue.

As I sat with Beth, I was reminded of a few things that had occurred prior to her first visit. When I returned her initial inquiry call, she mentioned that my voice message had been hard for her to hear. She had had trouble printing out my new patient intake form and had insisted I mail her a copy prior to her first visit. When I greeted her in my waiting room, she was flustered and frustrated because the only space in my office building's parking lot had been barely wide enough for her to open her car door. As she described her self-critical narrative, I made a mental note that Beth's Inner Critic was not limited to her own perceived flaws, but its criticism extended to the flaws of other situations and other people.

I asked Beth if she ever feels a reprieve from the "negative" voice. She responded that she probably does, but she couldn't give me an example. We considered shifting her description of the voice from a "negative" voice to a "critical" voice because it might allow her to see how disparaging and judgmental the voice was in her head. Sometimes if we can create a bit of space between ourselves and our Inner Critic, it helps create an opening for the birth of the Neutral Observer.

If Beth could begin to make a shift from identifying with her negative voice (I am negative, I am not interesting, I am unattractive) to seeing or observing her thoughts as critical comments directed at her (my thoughts are negative, my inner voice is telling me I am not interesting, my Inner Critic is commenting on my appearance), an important process can begin to take root. When we begin to observe our thoughts, we create the possibility that we don't identify with them or as them – maybe even we won't believe them. Our thoughts don't always have our best interests in mind.

I gave Beth a homework exercise – to begin to notice when her Inner Critic popped up and to observe her critical thoughts as if they were floating around her but were not a part of her.

She came to her second appointment very agitated, as she reported that the exercise was hard and frustrating. However, something she had come across on the internet seemed to corroborate the benefits of the exercise, and she said she was willing to stick with it.

Beth continued to reject the idea of bodywork, so we did a seated meditation that visit, where I talked her through a body scan; the scan gently guided her to feel and observe different parts of her body. She reported feeling a bit more relaxed and made another appointment – this time for bodywork.

At our next session, she lay down on my bodywork table. It took her a while to get settled on the table; the pillow under her knees was too bulky, and she was frustrated that my bodywork table was too high for her to get up comfortably. When I put my hands on her shoulders, she commented that my hands were cold. I gently took my hands away and rubbed them together a bit, and then I placed them back on her shoulders. After a few moments, we began to revisit the body scan we had done seated. This time lying on the table.

After a few more moments, she said, "I've noticed my critical voice is really busy." After a quiet pause, she continued, "It criticizes everything I do and everything others do. It's hard on me and hard on others."

I asked her if she could observe what she just said without judgment or criticism. "Yeah, maybe," she said. "Maybe I can." I guided her to feel what, if anything, might be going on in her body as she was observing herself. She said nothing in response. The session ended with some Neutral Observer homework, which she agreed to try... "maybe."

Beth's cancer treatment protocol was rigorous. She had a daughter who lived in New York City, and she decided to move in with her daughter and her daughter's family. It made sense for Beth to receive treatment at a hospital where she could simultaneously be cared for and supported by her family.

In our last session before she moved, she shared with me some insight from a new book that she had read and from our sessions together. Beth had begun to understand that her Inner Critic had ruled her life up until now. She had never challenged or questioned it; rather, she didn't see it as anything other than who she was. Beth had begun to see that she was more than her thoughts, and more than the "negative" voice in her head.

Beth lived for two more years with the help of her devoted daughter and family. She came back to see me twice during those years. She was in and out of treatment; her cancer became aggressive, and yet she was determined to beat it. Beth had worked on distancing herself from her Inner Critic. She had gained awareness, and she admitted to me that she was afraid.

Our last two visits were more intimate, so to speak, as she told me more about the struggles in her past and also about her tremendous love for her daughter and grandchildren. She wanted to spend what time she had left with the people she loved so dearly.

On our last visit together, we did not do bodywork. We talked the whole time. Sometimes, if a patient has a strong Inner Critic, they have a hard time seeing and acknowledging their own "fabulousness." That visit I wanted to share with Beth what I had seen and felt during our work together. I told her how brave and honest she was, how deeply thoughtful and curious she was, how strong she was, and how much I appreciated our conversations about all the books she had read. And what a privilege it was to know her.

YOUR THOUGHTS DON'T ALWAYS HAVE YOUR BACK

What does it mean that our thoughts don't have our back? While this may seem like a strange thing to say, let's explore for a minute the possibility that our thoughts may not always tell us the truth. Is it feasible that our thoughts may not be telling us or giving us the most accurate and well-meaning information about ourselves and the world around us?

The movie *A Beautiful Mind* offers an extreme representation of both the utter brilliance of a mind and the lies and delusions that a schizophrenic mind can conjure up. *A Beautiful Mind* details the life of prominent and brilliant mathematician John Nash, who develops paranoid schizophrenia. The characterization of John Nash in the movie illustrates what society celebrates most and fears most about the mind, all in one person. Mental illnesses, like schizophrenia, may present with distortions of and detachments from reality, but the phenomenon of the mind telling us things about ourselves – things that are baseless and false – is not limited to pathological conditions.

Our thoughts can derail us and, at times, thwart us in a way that is deeply paralyzing. I don't believe it to be an overstatement when I say that our thoughts at times are not simply distracting but can be disorienting, debilitating, and blatantly untrue. Many of the thoughts that rattle through my head are super unhelpful.

You need a nap, so you must be lazy. You need "me" time, so you aren't a good friend or a good mother. You missed your workout three days in a row, so you are undisciplined. What, you're hungry again, you just ate a little while ago. What's wrong with you?

This is just a mere sampling. The list of critical thoughts I can have about myself is pretty lengthy. I remember committing to an awareness assignment after attending a bodywork retreat, where I journaled my stream-of-consciousness thoughts every morning for a month. I skipped some days, but at the end of the month, I was shocked at the number of thoughts that were critical and "negative." It was certainly not helpful to be talking to myself like this every day.

But when I started to push back on my thoughts, it felt unnatural and unfamiliar. It felt wrong to question what my thoughts were telling me. I was never taught to question or challenge my thoughts. Were you? While I stopped the journaling practice after the month was over, the exercise made me more aware of the thoughts I woke up to. I know some people call it "waking up on the wrong side of the bed," but boy, if I'm being completely honest with myself, I can really wake up in a snit.

I had to accept that my thoughts don't always have my back. And I needed to do something constructive with that self-awareness. What I really needed was to learn to not believe all my thoughts and know the difference between ones that are critical and ones that are helpful. When I think, "You are unfair to your family when you need time to yourself," I need to know I'm being critical. When I think, "You should write a book about felt emotion," I should know I'm being brilliant. But I have to know the difference, and that is a challenge.

Questioning our thoughts is not commonplace in our world today, but I will challenge each of you to begin to do so. You could pick one or two thoughts a day and ask yourself, is this thought helpful, constructive, and self-affirming? Or is it hurtful, undermining, or self-loathing? In the experiential section at the end of this chapter, you can start a journaling practice like the one that offered me endless insight into my many thoughts.

I get it! Changing that Inner Critic into a Neutral Observer takes commitment, persistence, and patience. It can be so very hard. In challenging and questioning our thoughts, we are going up against an ever-present colossus; our thinking mind is everywhere and everything in our lives. In our goal-oriented world that moves at a breakneck pace, thoughts keep us going. They make stuff happen. They pay the bills. They get us into college. They put people on the moon. They create new technology and life-saving advancements. Rest assured, thoughts aren't going anywhere. Chances are they will always be the predominant way we interact in our world and with our world.

But if we can shift the way we "think" about "feeling" just a bit, we can give sitting with ourselves and our hard feelings a fighting chance. Just ponder, for a moment, that feeling has a place in our world, in your world. What that looks like and how we go about it lies in the pages ahead.

CHAPTER FOUR EXPERIENTIAL

I. BODY PLAY: QUIETING OUR MINDS AND SPENDING
    MORE TIME IN OUR BODIES

Let's play with the idea of living less in our minds and more in our bodies. We will explore staying with an inner experience, feeling, or sensation, while at the same time quieting our busy mind.

A common misconception about quieting the mind or meditating is that it involves NOT thinking. Quieting the mind is not the absence of thoughts; rather, it is a skill that involves observing our thoughts and distancing from them; distancing ourselves from our thoughts means that we resist getting wrapped up in, identifying with, or attaching to a thought. When we detach from our thoughts, we quiet our cognitive perseverating, obsessing, and ruminating. When we quiet the mind, we simply notice a thought and let it pass through us without attachment. This takes practice.

You can play with these two concepts separately or at the same time.

- **EXPLORE YOUR INNER EXPERIENCE:** Find a comfortable position and take a moment to feel your inhale and exhale. Shift your attention inward and allow your inner focus to land somewhere in your body. Some examples of where you might land are a sensation of hot or cold, a feeling of pain, discomfort, pleasure, or ease, an emotion, a palpable energy or pulse, your breath, an area of tension, or a tangible anxiety. Once you have landed in a feeling or sensation within your body, observe and explore that inner experience. Resist questioning whether you are doing it right. Simply stay with and feel this part of yourself.

- **QUIET THE MIND:** Notice if you are wrapped up in thoughts. Resist judgment, just notice. Resist attaching to a thought that may pop up (thoughts will indeed pop up) and gently shift your attention back to your body and your inner experience. Let your thoughts float through you or around you, but play with NOT attaching to them. Let thoughts float and gently bring your awareness back to the body. Stay with this practice for five to ten minutes. Set a timer if needed.

2. AWARENESS OF YOUR INNER CRITIC AND THE BIRTH OF YOUR NEUTRAL OBSERVER

By gaining an awareness of your Inner Critic, you can create an opening for the birth of your Neutral Observer. Being able to identify and label your Inner Critic allows you insight into your inner voice that comments, critiques, and judges.

With this insight comes the realization that there is an alternative. There is another way! Your Neutral Observer is very different from your critical inner voice. It is a constructive way to approach viewing yourself. Let's play with these concepts a bit. Let's practice catching your Inner Critic hard at work, and then let's welcome in your Neutral Observer.

- **AWARENESS OF YOUR INNER CRITIC:** If you can begin to spot your Inner Critic on the fly during your day, you can simply take note of how often it visits you and the kind of comments it makes. In addition, you can commit to journaling your critical thoughts daily. By simply keeping a notebook handy and jotting them down as you notice them, you begin to get a sense of how busy and how tenacious your Inner Critic is. What does your Inner Critic tell you? How often does it visit? Can you spot when your Inner Critic is rearing its head?

- **THE BIRTH OF THE NEUTRAL OBSERVER:** Begin to play with the idea of observing. What does it mean to simply observe – your thoughts, your actions, your conversations, your behaviors, your inner experience, your breath, your feelings? Resist verbal commentary. Your Neutral Observer is a quiet presence that exists separate from your thoughts. It is an inner eye or inner lens that you notice yourself through. Notice. Observe. Nothing else. Detach from your thoughts. This is the birth of your Neutral Observer, and it is profound!

3. "MY EXPERIENCE OF FEELING EMOTIONS AS A CHILD" PROMPT

Choose one of these two statements as a springboard for a journal entry, a painting/picture, a meditation, a poem, a song, a dance, or any form of creative expression.

My upbringing/caregivers encouraged me to feel my emotions by...

My upbringing/caregivers discouraged me from feeling my emotions by...

CHAPTER FIVE

AVOIDING, NUMBING, AND DISTRACTING

My tendency was to push painful feelings away, to hide from them. I became an expert at evading my feelings and avoiding situations that might cause feelings. I swallowed my feelings; food became a way I both numbed and soothed myself. I disappeared into my room or apartment to avoid interaction and connection. I busied myself with doing things that kept my mind off hard feelings, like working, cleaning, studying, exercising, shopping, or watching TV. I escaped my feelings in any way possible. At least I was safe – safe from feeling, that is.

WE AVOID THINGS THAT CAUSE US PAIN

We are hardwired to recoil from those things in life that cause us pain. It is an innate response. We instinctively move our hand away from a hot stove or a boiling pot that threatens to burn us. We jump back from a fast-moving car that speeds narrowly close to us as we wait at a street corner. We instinctively run or hide from danger.

Like danger, we move away from felt emotion too – from difficult feelings and emotional pain. Just like we recoil from a hot stove, we retreat from feelings of rejection and humiliation. Like we might duck to avoid the swing of a fist coming our way, we duck and swerve as strong feelings of loneliness or shame roll into our bodies. When we are fearful for our life, we freeze or fight or flee. That fear can be felt in our bodies (felt emotion), and we simultaneously shut down, tense up, or run.

We inherently know that some emotions can be painful – very painful. Consequently, we create ways to anticipate them, avoid them, and hide from them. For the purpose of categorizing ways in which we evade felt emotion, I have divided our avoiding propensities into four groups.

- RETREATING: We create habits and behaviors that keep us away from people and situations that might stir or create challenging felt emotion within us.
- PROTECTING: We tense our muscles and hold our breath in an attempt to stop or limit felt emotion.

- NUMBING: We find ways to numb feelings inside of us, including but not limited to food, alcohol, and prescription or recreational drugs.
- DISTRACTING: We engage in activities and behaviors that distract us from the present moment of our felt emotion, for example scrolling through our smartphones, playing video games, excessive shopping or exercise, and mindlessly eating. We can stay busy with cleaning, organizing, and working to distract ourselves too.

But when we move away from emotional pain, we don't always simply step back, like we step back from a hot stove. Instead, we may run away, as fast as we can, in the opposite direction. And the opposite direction of feeling is not feeling. In this case, we don't want to feel anything at all, so we numb ourselves in any way we can.

If we burn our hand often enough, there is a chance we might avoid cooking altogether. If we experience emotional pain often enough, there is a chance we may find a way to stop feeling altogether. This may seem like a radical or maybe ridiculous statement, but we can and do, in fact, make an unconscious choice, and sometimes a conscious choice, not to feel.

Remember, we not only run from our difficult thoughts and narratives, but we run from our painful felt emotion too. If we can understand and acknowledge that recoiling from felt emotion is a common reflex, we are armed with a new self-awareness, and we can begin to notice when we run and hide from emotional pain. With this self-awareness, we can begin to connect the dots between avoiding our emotions and the choices we make and the behaviors we engage in. Our unwillingness to tolerate painful and challenging feelings limits our ability to take risks, make mistakes, make commitments, and throw ourselves into new and exciting adventures. Our inability to tolerate painful and challenging feelings contributes to our reliance on distractions, substances, and the myriad behaviors that help us avoid and numb ourselves.

NOT FEELING IT – EVADING FEELINGS

These days, most people would agree that it is better to acknowledge, discuss, and feel our emotions, as opposed to ignoring or avoiding them. I am not making any grand or novel statement when I say it is beneficial for us to feel our feelings instead of denying, numbing, or swallowing them.

Of course, we are not always able or available to feel every little feeling that comes our way. Sometimes, we need to push away a nagging worry when we have to get a job done or meet a deadline. Sometimes, we have to push through feelings, like fear for example, to actually make changes and take risks in our lives. If we stopped and paid attention to every emotion that came upon us, we would be very busy indeed and perhaps very unproductive. Consider...

- You just got yelled at by your boss, and yet you are expected at a two o'clock meeting.
- You got in a fight with your boyfriend, but you're about to take an important exam.

- You just found out that a friend is very ill, and you are rushing to the airport to catch a flight.

Momentarily setting aside a feeling is not avoiding or numbing a feeling. When we make a conscious choice to reject a particular feeling, we are acting with intention in our lives. In essence, we are saying to ourselves, "I am choosing to blow past this feeling of fear because my resistance to change is holding me back from getting the degree I want or the job I desire." When we must finish a deadline at work, we may need to shelve our feeling of inadequacy or insecurity because finishing that task assures us that we have a livelihood and an income.

Sometimes feelings can be so powerful and plentiful that they feel paralyzing, and if we let ourselves become immobilized by them, our lives suffer. But take note that the important factor here is that we are mindful that we are shelving or pushing through feelings. When we mindlessly avoid feelings, we are never looping back to check in with them, and when we don't check back in, we lose important information about our human-ness and our emotional life.

Avoiding and numbing is not intentional and not mindful. Have you ever had a strong, bothersome, or unwanted feeling wash upon you, and you immediately started scrolling through your emails, or maybe you decided to clean out a cupboard? Or maybe you grabbed a conveniently located bag of chips or visited the vending machine at work? Or perhaps reached for a glass of wine or beer? Avoiding a feeling can be so commonplace and habitual for us that we barely take note of our behavior. We get very used to pushing our feelings down instead of feeling them because we live busy lives. Felt emotion is a bother; it is a nuisance. We don't have time to stop and stay with a feeling.

Can you remember the last time felt emotion visited you? Can you remember a time when you had a nagging or tugging feeling inside? Maybe a burning in your belly or the sensation that you were punched in the stomach? Or maybe an undeniable feeling of dread?

Ugh. Not dread again. Really? Dread visits me on rare occasions, usually before a big exam that I feel unprepared for or before a social situation that promises to be both awkward and overwhelming. When dread pays me a social call, it starts just below my sternum as a dank heaviness and slowly moves downward. Once dread makes its way to my core, it transforms into a heavy hollowing deep inside me. Dread likes to hang out and always overstays its welcome. It feels triumphant when I cancel my plans and stay home eating ice cream. But when I decide to feel my dread and do what I'm dreading anyway, it loses its footing and its power. My dread will then slowly fade away.

When felt emotion is both undeniable and uncomfortable, quite frankly, the last thing we want to do is feel it. When was the last time you felt like being punched in the gut and then letting that feeling hang around so you could really take it in and feel it? I'm sure that sounds like the absolute last thing in the world you would voluntarily choose to do. Ridiculous, right?

But wait! Remember our Frequent Feeler Miles? Oh yes, I remember, there are some rewards involved with sitting with difficult felt emotion. So, the question becomes: do we sit with the hard feelings, or do we choose a behavior that takes the edge off and maybe pushes the feeling away for another day? Or maybe something that can numb it altogether?

- When was the last time in your recent memory that you sat with an uncomfortable or painful feeling?
- If a bothersome feeling followed you home from work, did you take five minutes and sit quietly with the feeling? Did you get to know the feeling a bit, see where it is sitting in your body, and maybe explore exactly what it feels like?
- If something is brewing during your day, would you take time to acknowledge the feeling and stay with it long enough to see if it lessens, changes, or passes?

If these questions are hard to answer, you are not alone. If these questions feel silly, odd, strange, or weird, you are far from alone. Sitting with hard feelings is pretty rare these days. With so many things to take our minds off our feelings, we don't need to know how to stay with them. But this is problematic.

PENNY: I FELT PAIN ON MY OWN TERMS

Penny was a young woman in her mid-twenties with a history of anorexia and self-harm. She had struggled with anorexia for much of high school and started to cut herself her junior year. When she came to my office, Penny had had extensive psychotherapy and a transformative few months in an eating disorder program; she had neither harmed herself nor restricted her calorie intake for close to five years. She had graduated college with honors and had just started her second post-college job.

This job, which she once believed would be her dream job, had turned out to be extremely stressful. Her boss was super tough on her, and she was feeling overwhelmed and stuck. She was thinking about cutting again. Her therapist recognized that Penny was "somatic," meaning that she felt things in her body strongly and powerfully. Her therapist was eager for her to understand how to manage and cope with such strong somatic feelings, and recommended she see me for bodywork.

Penny was up for jumping right into bodywork. She lay on my table during her first session and shared an enormous amount of insight into how she felt both insecurity and doubt in her body. She needed just a small amount of guidance to flesh out what those feelings felt like; she was ripe for a deeper understanding and knowledge of the strength and shape of her felt emotion.

During our fourth bodywork session, she told me she hadn't thought about cutting herself in the past few weeks. I asked her what she thought might be different, and quite frankly, her insight blew me away.

"You know, I think I would cut in high school because I didn't want to feel all my feelings, especially my feelings of rejection. My friends weren't really friends. Some were okay. Some were pretty cruel to me." Penny continued, "I never realized it before, but cutting was my way of controlling when I felt pain. I didn't want to feel the cruelty of my friends. I felt pain on my own terms."

Penny's understanding and interpretation of her experience with self-harm was profound. Her words "I felt pain on my own terms" reverberated with a gravity that moved us both deeply. When we feel out of control in our lives, sometimes we try to gain control over how much we eat or drink, how much we exercise, or how much we weigh. When we feel powerless, sometimes we try to find power over our bodies. When we don't want to feel our emotional pain, sometimes we create different pain, so at least we know it or know when to expect it. At least it is on our own terms.

Penny's story suggests that when we can acknowledge that we feel emotion in our bodies, in a big way, we have more control over our experiences and feelings because we understand them — often for the first time in our lives. I am always struck when a patient tells me that they had never even thought about their felt emotion before — never. For Penny, despite being a Frequent Feeler, she had never paid much attention to her powerful felt emotion or realized that those feelings may have influenced how she existed in the world.

We are not able to control many things in life – the families we grow up in, the ways we are treated, the experiences or traumas that happen to us – but we will still feel those things deeply and profoundly. Penny gave herself permission to understand what it meant to be a somatic feeler, and being a somatic feeler validated everything about who she was in the world. "I feel things in a huge way. My emotional pain can be hugely painful."

Her level of insight deepened with her deeper understanding of herself. She began to understand that she never learned how to sit with her emotional pain, and she never learned to trust that the pain would pass or that she could get to the other side of that pain. Through bodywork, she began to understand her self-harm behaviors in a way that made her struggles make more sense. That insight was the motivation behind her wanting to learn to stay with and feel her feelings more and more. And for Penny, the need or compulsion to create or control her pain, by causing herself pain, diminished.

BODY BREAK

Let's take a moment to notice ourselves. Do a brief check-in with your body. Are you feeling tension anywhere in particular? Your jaw? Your neck or shoulders? Your hands? Your hips? Your toes? Simply notice.

For a minute or two, bring a very soft and gentle breath into the tension you are feeling. Yes, breathe into your jaw, your hips, your toes. Resist questioning how odd that sounds or that it may be anatomically impossible. Instead, embrace the visualization and imagine an easy and soft breath moving into your tension, wherever that may be. That's all.

MERE DISTRACTION OR A MODERN-DAY CRISIS?

When the reality of an ever-increasing number of distractions, some literally at our fingertips, meets the human tendency to want to avoid difficult feelings, the result is, more often than not, the shifting of our attention from feeling to something else. We'll take any excuse to do anything other than sitting with our pesky, nagging, and difficult feelings, and presto, we don't have to feel them. Add into the mix our society's emphasis on doing and achieving and our long to-do lists and, quite honestly, the idea of being present with what we are feeling is just left in the dust. As a result, we have older and newer generations that can't sit with themselves. And hence, we have a modern-day crisis.

Remember when we used to sit in a doctor's waiting room and read a magazine and maybe take a few breaths before being called in? Remember when we would stand in the grocery store checkout line and simply be with our thoughts or feelings for a few quick moments? Why did we do this? Because we didn't have anything else to do in those moments. We were held captive in our own present moment. Now things are very different. Anyone else checking email or doing work in the grocery line and waiting room these days?

Sitting on the subway or bus, waiting at an airport gate to board a plane, and sitting in a theater, classroom, or boardroom waiting for the next event to start were all little gems of time where we could check in with ourselves. Now, more often than not, we are checking in with and responding to our texts, emails, and social media instead.

If we are struggling to sit with ourselves in the grocery line or on the subway, as these are moments of relative calm, how can we expect to sit with ourselves in moments of chaos, anxiety, or panic? What does it say that we are struggling to stay present with our pleasant feelings too? We rarely let ourselves bask in "good" feelings, like appreciation or gratitude, let alone "hard" feelings, like rejection and shame. We push on to the next thing regardless of whether the feeling is wonderful or challenging.

Do you sit with or stay with lovely or pleasant feelings?

* When someone gives you a compliment or recognizes an accomplishment, do you believe it? Can you?
* When you see a beautiful sunset, do you stop to appreciate it? Can you?
* When a friend greets you with a hug, do you feel the warmth and caring that is coming your way? Can you?
* When was the last time you sat with yourself when you were feeling fulfilled or acknowledged?
* How often do you immediately get gobbled up by chores that grasp, demand, or distract your attention, even when you have a really nice feeling to let in?

In other words, a lot of the time we don't bask in the small pearls of feeling that might otherwise fill us up. By the same token, we rarely take advantage of downtime the way we used to. Instead, we are quick to fill our quiet moments with stuff to do and stuff to take our minds off other stuff. It is a rare occurrence when we stop and take in a moment anymore. And if we can't take in a relatively enjoyable moment – or even an exceptional or breathtaking moment – our hard moments don't stand a chance.

When we reach for our smartphone, chocolate, a glass of wine, a video game, or the TV remote, we may be expressing an underlying desire to be distracted or numbed – or both. Distraction can feel good or even really, really, really good; it can also feel fairly neutral.

Often, we are not conscious that we are shifting our attention or focus from an uncomfortable feeling or undesired thought to something different. We may be bored and are unconsciously looking for a distraction. We may not want to be ruminating or perseverating, so we want out of our own heads. We may not want to feel the felt emotions that are popping up, so we want out of our bodies. Simply put, we just want out sometimes! Sometimes the feelings in our present moment are simply unbearable. And we will do whatever it takes to get out of ourselves.

When feelings are more than we think we can handle, we will seek all manner of behaviors to get away from the feelings. It is no revelation that avoiding and numbing feelings play a role in eating disorders, addiction, self-harm as well as other mental illnesses. Emotional pain and difficult feelings have always contributed to mental health disorders, and, of course, looking at and understanding these difficult feelings play a role in mental health therapies and treatment.

As we look through the lens of felt emotion, we build on an existing understanding and acknowledgment of numbing and distracting; the concept of felt emotion is critical to understanding why individuals seek to numb or redirect painful feelings. The recognition that one can tolerate painful emotions by feeling them – in the body – has a role to play in the treatment of mental health struggles. Experiencing painful feelings and knowing that we can ride them, feel them, and get through them – through staying connected to them in the body – is vital to the conscious decision to not engage in a harmful or addictive behavior. Remember, we can use felt emotion as a discernible inner experience that is real and tangible within us. Your felt emotion is not a vague or abstract concept. It has shape, intensity, and density within you.

Indeed, we can understand that what at first appears to be just a trend in our modern, fast-paced world — where we are enticed by distraction and avoid our feelings — is actually more damaging and problematic at its core. Not knowing how to sit with tough feelings plays out across all manner of behavioral and mental health struggles.

We can connect the dots: a culture or a generation that does not know how to sit with their challenging feelings learns quickly and adaptively that they don't have to sit with those feelings because alternatives to feeling emotional pain abound. The alternatives to feeling emotional pain are many, some more harmful and addictive than others. In order to learn to tolerate and ride out our tough feelings, we can gain tools to stay with our feelings, be present, and move toward ourselves. So how do we do this? Onward to Part Two.

CHAPTER FIVE EXPERIENTIAL

I. BODY PLAY: A 50/50 MINDFULNESS PRACTICE

The intention of this exercise is to play with the idea of feeling your body and staying with yourself during daily tasks and simple conversations. We tend to lose a connection to ourselves when we are going about our day, but we can indeed stay in our bodies and connected to ourselves during everyday experiences. It just takes practice.

- Can you feel your feet when talking to a friend or coworker?
- Can you notice your breath while checking out at the grocery store?
- Can you soften your shoulders while working at the computer?
- Can you quiet your thoughts while walking to the car, bus, or train?
- Can you release your jaw while looking at your phone?

These are all opportunities during your everyday life to put half of your attention on your inner experience while placing the other half of your attention on doing a particular task. We all know the phrase "walk and chew gum at the same time." Well, this is exactly that.

Simply bring half of your attention to your inner experience while going about your day. Can you keep 50% of your attention on your feet while you wash your hands? Can you have 50% of your inner focus on your breath while you check your emails?

Remember, this takes practice. At first glance, this exercise appears easy. It is not. It takes baby steps and commitment.

2. CAN YOU PAUSE... AND TAKE IN A MEANINGFUL, JOYFUL, OR BEAUTIFUL MOMENT? AND WHAT DOES THAT FEEL LIKE IN YOUR BODY?

The next time you experience a moment of appreciation, gratitude, awe, satisfaction, amusement, or love...

- Can you PAUSE... give yourself permission to take a beat and take it in?
- Can you experience the power of this moment from within? What does it feel like in your body? Does it take your breath away? Does warmth spread from your core or heart? Does it feel effortful or hard? Does it feel like a waste of time? Does it feel deep or spiritual? What does it feel like? Don't judge. Just feel.

3. "HOW I AVOID MY FEELINGS" PROMPT

Use this statement as a springboard for a journal entry, a painting/picture, a meditation, a poem, a song, a dance, or any form of creative expression. Be gentle and nonjudgmental with yourself, and at the same time, be candid and forthcoming. Remember to be specific — naming, identifying, and describing the behaviors you engage in to move away from a feeling.

I avoid my painful feelings and uncomfortable felt emotion by...

EXPERIENTIAL

PART TWO

A SOLUTION

CHAPTER SIX

CHOOSING MINDFULNESS OVER MINDLESSNESS

I couldn't sit with myself. I found all manners of distractions and numbing behaviors. Food, excessive exercise, isolating from social situations, and retreating from friendships and relationships became my way of protecting myself. If I didn't engage or interact with the world, I would surely not have to feel much of anything. And so, I became numb to the world around me. And to myself.

This was no way to live.

Distractions abound in our modern world. But we have a choice – a choice between living a mindful existence or a mindless existence. Of course, it is never just one or the other. And it is not as simple as it may seem. We may live mindfully in some aspects of our lives and yet have little intention in other areas. But understanding the difference and being able to distinguish between mindful and mindless behaviors and choices is a necessary self-awareness. The more mindful we are, the more present we are.

Make no mistake, what we are learning to do in this book does not occur without mindful intention and a willingness to be in the present moment. Making the conscious decision to begin to sit with hard, uncomfortable feelings, and at times painful or excruciating ones, is a mindful choice, one that can only be made with purpose and commitment. Why otherwise would we willingly choose to be vulnerable and feel tough feelings? Because there is no getting through emotional pain without the mindful intention to do so.

TO WHAT AND WHERE DOES YOUR ATTENTION GO?

A number of years ago, I went to a morning workshop with a Hindu priest. His name was Dandapani, and I have never forgotten this quote from his session: "Where awareness goes, energy flows." Dandapani is the author of *The Power of Unwavering Focus*, and his presentation that day connected the dots between the things we both consciously and unconsciously direct our attention to and what we place importance and meaning on. If we direct our attention to our anxieties and worries, that is where our energy will go. If we focus on our worries, that is who we become, so to speak. If our thoughts are full of fear, we are fearful. If our thoughts are critical, we are critical.

But Dandapani inspired great hope in each one of us at his workshop. He explained that it is indeed within our power – our willpower actually – to direct our attention to the things that are important to us, to the things we want in our lives. His words that morning left an indelible mark on me.

After attending his workshop, I began to take notice of where my attention would go. This workshop coincided with a time in my family's life when we were readying ourselves to move abroad. In just a few short months, we would be living overseas. The day after the workshop, I set aside fifteen minutes for a quiet meditation, and I observed that my attention went to an alarming number of different things...

- How worried I was about leaving my medical practice
- How hungry I was because I hadn't had time to eat lunch
- How stressed out I was feeling about my kids starting a new school
- How anxious I was about not sleeping well due to all that was on my mind
- How in the world I would pack up our lives into just suitcases
- How my back hurt, and my spine felt crooked

- Oh yes, I needed to remember to pick up milk and strawberries from the grocery store, and my daughter had a doctor's appointment later

I was overwhelmed by so many things that needed my attention. One after another, my attention jumped from one worry to the next nagging feeling, to the thing that I couldn't forget, to my hunger, and back to another worry. My attention was consumed with worries, to-do lists, and my own physical discomfort. With my attention flowing in so many different directions and to so many different distresses, no wonder I felt so ungrounded and unsettled. I was indeed becoming all of my worried thoughts.

The things that we choose to do or surround ourselves with can either grasp, demand, or distract our attention. Replying to an email from your boss may demand your attention because an immediate response is required. Taking a run may demand your attention because it is important to you to stay fit. Watching a movie may grasp your attention because it is intriguing or humorous, while playing a game on your smartphone may distract your attention because you are bored or possibly avoiding doing the dishes. Eating a pint of ice cream may grasp and distract your attention because it tastes so delicious, and maybe you are avoiding an anxious feeling. These are all examples of where we place our attention, and we may notice that some are healthier or more constructive than others.

A mindful behavior is one we bring our full intention to. For example, if we have the intention to calm our minds and move our bodies, we may engage in a daily yoga practice. A mindless behavior does not have an intent or purpose behind it; often mindless behaviors are unconscious. When we are unaware or unconscious of a shift in attention, like when we reach for our phones when we are bored or grab a candy bar when we are stressed, we do so mostly without thought or consideration.

We distinguish between mindless and mindful practices and behaviors so we can begin to take note of where our attention is going at any given moment and how to tell the difference between the two. The more we can be mindful about where we direct our attention, the more presence and intention we bring to our lives.

So where does all this fit into felt emotion, our feeling muscle, and our ability to feel or not feel our emotions? Well, every time we shift from a feeling surfacing to a behavior that takes us away from that feeling, we are moving away from ourselves and our present moment. If, as we read through these pages, we have committed to feeling more freely and fully, we will begin to realize that where our attention or focus goes is truly within our control; we can then understand that focusing on our feelings in any given moment is indeed a possible choice. Thus, we can begin to choose feeling, with intention and purpose, over engaging in a mindless distraction.

TARA: MAYBE I RUN FROM MYSELF SOMETIMES

Tara came to my office early in my career. She had been living and working on the Upper West Side of Manhattan on September 11, 2001, and had been significantly affected by the events of that day. She had witnessed friends and neighbors coming home from lower Manhattan covered in the dust of the fallen buildings, and like many, she had internalized all the terror and loss of life that day.

Tara told me this part of her history on our first visit. She was now living in Connecticut but still reliving the memories of that day. She also explained that she was struggling with a binge eating disorder, and she reported that she was binging on both sugary and salty foods almost every evening after work.

Tara told me with great frustration in her voice that she had been seeing a therapist for the past two years since moving to Connecticut, and yet her binging continued. She had made connections between her overeating and how it distracted her from her feelings of terror, guilt, and fear surrounding 9/11. She had recently read an article about mindfulness and eating, and was interested in learning more, but she admitted that she didn't know where to start.

Tara was an avid runner and had recently been sidelined by an ankle injury. She was beside herself with restlessness because running was a huge and important way that she dealt with her stress. She told me, "I literally do not know what to do with myself. I am so anxious and restless without running in my life. I'm eating all the time."

She told me point-blank that she was not interested in bodywork. I responded that I could give her some exercises and some homework to begin a mindfulness practice, but that my work did involve exploration of our body's inner experience, which would eventually mean bringing her attention inward and to her body. She left my office with some suggestions for journaling as well as an awareness exercise around her sensations of satiety and hunger.

Tara did make a follow-up appointment; however, she called a week later and cancelled.

Roughly two years later, I got a call from Tara. She wanted to come in for a visit, and she had some questions for me. When she came in, she was noticeably calmer and more grounded than her last visit. She told me her ankle had completely healed, and she was running again. She was so thankful to be running. She was still struggling with her binging in the evenings, and she was still seeing her therapist.

Her therapist had made a comment recently that had perplexed her, and she wanted to run it by me. "My therapist mentioned that my running, while great in so many ways, might also be a way I distract myself from feelings and memories of 9/11."

I remember thinking to myself, "Wow, this is really insightful. And yet it must also be hard for Tara to hear and digest." I was impressed with her wanting to consider this idea, as people are rarely willing to look at and challenge something so important to them.

Tara was still not interested in bodywork, so on this visit, we simply talked. We talked about how restless she had been when she couldn't run. And while it was clear that running was a great outlet for her stress and a terrific way for her to stay healthy and in shape, sometimes it did feel to her like she was "escaping" a bit when she was running. I asked her to explain more about her choice of the word "escaping."

"When I couldn't run, I could not sit still. I paced my apartment," Tara said. "I played games on my computer. I watched TV. I ate and I ate. It felt like I was in prison."

She repeated the word "prison," and then continued. "Running is great for me. I know that. But it also gives me something to do with myself. I struggle just being with myself. And I saw that it in a big way when I couldn't run."

I asked her what she thought of the idea of just sitting quietly for five to ten minutes with her feelings and thoughts. "Terrifying," she said, partly joking and partly dead serious. After a pause, she asked, "Are you being serious?" She looked at me like I had three heads.

I floated my interpretation of what I thought her therapist might have been referring to. I started with the possibility that we sometimes run away from our thoughts and our feelings by distracting ourselves. "Our thoughts and feelings can be so hard to be with sometimes. Even though running is great for you, it still might be a way you run from yourself too. Those two things can be true at the same time."

The Frequent Feeler in me held my breath, as I anticipated my words being hard for Tara to hear, and I contemplated that my words might generate defensiveness or even anger in Tara.

Instead, she was quiet for a few minutes. She appeared deep in thought. After a time, she said softly, "Yeah, maybe I run from myself sometimes." This felt big for Tara.

We sat quietly together for a few more minutes. The visit was coming to a close, and I wanted to end with what I hoped would feel like validation. "Sometimes our thoughts and feelings are really hard to sit with." I continued, "And we'd prefer to be doing something else."

Tara nodded quietly.

There was so much in that visit for Tara (and me) to digest and unpack. As I said earlier, this encounter happened early in my clinical career, and I have to admit it was a profound moment for me. I saw the impact of being both kind and honest with someone. I admired Tara's therapist for broaching the subject of her running having both a healthy impact as well as playing the role of a possible distraction or escape. Remember that as a Frequent Feeler I had spent my life avoiding conflict. But I realized that to be an effective doctor, I would have to have conversations that might be hard. I would need to sit with the feelings that would come up for both my patients and me. This was big for me too.

Tara would come back to my office, off and on, for many years. She eventually did try bodywork, and she saw both how it was really hard to sit with herself and how it also felt okay at times. And some days it was both hard and okay. Two things can be true at the same time.

DOES THIS BEHAVIOR MOVE YOU TOWARD OR AWAY FROM YOURSELF? AND WHAT DOES THAT MEAN?

To stay with our hard feelings, we must make a mindful choice to do so. In Tara's case above, she made a decision, one with purpose and intention, to stay with her hard thoughts and feelings. She identified her eating habits as a way she distracted herself, and she also acknowledged that her running, while immensely important to both her physical and mental health, was also occasionally an escape from difficult feelings and memories.

When Tara was unaware of the distracting nature of these behaviors, she was mindlessly engaging in them, but that changed when she brought awareness to her actions. It is important to understand that bringing awareness to an unwanted and sometimes mindless behavior (like Tara's binge eating) does not make it miraculously go away; behaviors take time and work to change, but awareness does open the door for making different choices and nurturing new behaviors.

So how do we go about identifying and acknowledging when we are mindless and when we are mindful? How we spend our time, the activities we choose to engage in, and the relationships and connections we pursue are all impacted by distraction. Sometimes, we are not even aware that a daily behavior or action distracts us because it has become so much a part of our habit or routine.

Maybe checking our phones endlessly throughout the day has become a habit, but are there times when it is a distraction? Sure.

This might be a great time to revisit and remember your Neutral Observer and your Inner Critic. When you engage in a mindful exercise, where you are asking yourself to be open and honest, it is helpful to enlist and align yourself with your Neutral Observer. Your Neutral Observer is a much better partner in looking at behaviors and choices with honesty (and kindness and acceptance) than your Inner Critic. Remember, your Inner Critic speaks to you from a place of fear and insecurity.

Another benefit of joining forces with your Neutral Observer is that it will help you refrain from categorizing your distractions as either "good" or "bad." Distractions have their place. Distractions get us out of our heads, and getting out of our heads is super helpful when we are ruminating, spiraling, and obsessing. Distractions are downtime, and downtime is important. Sometimes my all-important "me time" is pure distraction; I am aware of it, and for a bit of time, I unapologetically enjoy a word game on my phone or a good movie. No judgment, just enjoyment and a little escape from my day.

I would be remiss if I did not acknowledge that what might be a mere distraction for one person might be a huge time suck for another or a true addiction for someone else. An activity that may allow one individual to wind down at the end of a long work week might be a real obstacle and challenge to another's ability to live a functional and healthy life. Distractions must be looked at with clarity and candor, but also with deep empathy and understanding – and knowing that behaviors can derail and destroy people's lives. While we may want nothing more than to be present and engaged in our life, we accept that aspects of our lives can get out of our control and that we need to ask for help when that is the case.

A helpful way to gauge whether a behavior or choice that we make on a daily basis is a distraction or one that we make with intention (or maybe a combination of the two) is to ask whether these behaviors and choices bring us closer to or farther away from ourselves. This simple question, although not so simple indeed, helps us understand what things in our lives move us closer to the present moment, closer to our goals and purpose, and closer to connection and fulfillment. And conversely, when we answer this question honestly and without judgment, we discover the things in our lives that do not.

What does it mean for something to bring you closer to yourself? Well, you have to know yourself in order to answer this question, and you have to be open and honest with yourself to answer this question fully and forthrightly. If you want to begin identifying the things that distract your attention and distract you from living the life you want, you need to be clear about your greater goals in life.

- Do you want purpose and meaning in your life?
- Do you want connection, relationships, and love?
- Do you want to be present and engaged in your life?

- Do you want financial success and recognition?
- Do you want health and contentment?

Maybe you want it all and more! Once you have a good sense of the things that you desire in life, the things that you want to make happen in your life, and/or the things you want to prioritize in your life, you can ask these questions of your choices and behaviors:

- Does this behavior enhance what I consider to be purposeful and important in my life? Does this activity divert my attention away from what is purposeful and important in my life?
- Does this choice take me out of the present moment?
- Does this activity replenish and/or restore important resources within me to continue living my life with vitality and purpose?
- Does this behavior or activity bring me closer to the people who are important and meaningful to me?
- Is this choice, behavior, or action a mixture of both? (Meaning it can EITHER bring me closer to myself while moving me farther from the significant people in my life OR bring me away from myself but closer to the significant people in my life). Remember, two things can be true at the same time.

You may wonder why I ask whether the activity or behavior brings you closer to or farther away from the important people in your life. The reason is twofold. Firstly, living a present, mindful, and purposeful life does not happen in a bubble. We are creatures who thrive and grow with connection, touch, love, and community. Secondly, factoring in how our behaviors affect those closest to us helps us live thoughtfully and mindfully aware of the consequences of our actions. So, when you assess your life and the choices you make, the data you collect must be looked at in relationship to how present and connected you are to those people whom you hold dear.

When you fold into the equation how your choices and behaviors impact your relationships, the result may not be as clear or clean as you might hope. Sometimes checking your phone, even though your family is asking for your attention, can't be avoided. There is an emergency at work or an email that requires an immediate response; responding to this email might be moving you closer to your goals of more recognition at work or simply ensuring that you keep your job. And still your family is annoyed at you and continues to need your attention. At the risk of sounding like a broken record, two things can be true at the same time. Don't judge; simply take note (and remember to enlist your Neutral Observer).

Doug was a patient of mine and a dad of two young children. He loved sports cars and spent a few hours every Sunday driving his own sports car to various locations around the state. He told me it was one of the few things that gave him true pleasure in his life. Doug's wife was convinced that it was a convenient way to avoid the chaos of his family life. In a moment of honesty, he told me that there was some truth in his wife's accusation. But that didn't change the fact that his rides were immensely important to him. Both things were true for him.

In the experiential exercises at the end of this chapter, you will have the opportunity to explore and journal (with openness and willingness) where, how, and when you are moving toward yourself and where, how, and when you are moving away from yourself. If you can do this candidly and without judgment, you will gain important insight into how you can align with your life goals.

When you view your desire and commitment to feel freely and fully – both your hard and wonderful felt emotions – through the lens of moving closer to yourself and others, you see that feeling is a choice you can make. By committing to tolerating and staying with hard feelings, you are acknowledging that two things are true at the same time; you are recognizing that a feeling is hard, uncomfortable, and maybe even painful, and yet you are resolute in your willingness to stay with it and outlast it.

BODY BREAK

Place the book down, and if you are able, stand up (this exercise can easily be done seated if need be). Gently begin to jiggle or shake your hands (adjust to accommodate your range of motion or any pain or injuries you might have). As you shake your hands, feel the energy that is generated in your hands, wrists, and arms. After a minute, stop the shaking or jiggling and continue to feel that energy. As the energy dissipates, continue to feel your arms, wrists, and hands as you pick the book up again. That's all.

THE PRESENT MOMENT IS FLEETING
AND EVER-CHANGING

Not only does being mindful bring us into the present and closer to ourselves, but it allows us to embrace some universal truths about the present moment. You may recall in Chapter Three, we talked about felt emotion being an inner truth for us because it is an inner experience in real time – felt emotion is our present moment. Whether our present moment feels joyful, painful, content, or uncomfortable, it is our valid inner experience in that particular moment.

There is a funny thing about the present moment… there is always another moment to follow it, another opportunity to be present right around the bend. When we choose mindfulness over mindlessness, we are accepting and embracing the notion that each moment is an exquisite opportunity to awaken to our human experience. And the opportunities to do so abound — because there are a lot of moments in an hour, a day, a month, a year, a lifetime.

I remember a bodywork session with Josh, who had recently lost a job. He was remarking that his mood had been unpredictably up and down during the past week. One minute, he was fearful of not making rent. The next moment he was thankful not to have to interact with a difficult coworker anymore. At night Josh would lie awake worrying about health insurance. During our bodywork session, he noted that maybe this job loss was an opportunity to do something really meaningful with his life. Josh was considering going back to school and moving his career in a completely different direction.

His feeling muscle was busy, and his moments were changing at a breakneck pace. His moments, his thoughts, and his feelings were shapeshifting rapidly.

There is an inherent gift that we receive when we embrace mindfulness and awaken to the present moment, and that gift is the realization and the insight that our moments are dynamic and impermanent. What we are experiencing in one moment might be very different from the next moment. And that is worth both recognizing and appreciating. Why is this a gift, you might ask? Well, we gain the insight that moments don't last forever. And similarly, feelings don't last forever. A single feeling is not a permanent state of being.

As I'm writing this, I am reminded of a conversation that I had with a wise older friend. I was conflicted over going to naturopathic medical school and all the years of schooling that lay ahead of me after giving up dance. "By the time I complete my premed requirements, finish medical school, and pass all the clinical and board requirements, I will be in my thirties," I told her with a combination of apprehension and utter defeat in my voice.

I'll never forget her short response that left me without a retort. "Well, you'll be in your thirties either way, so why not be in your thirties and be a doctor?" she questioned.

Um, yes, she was right, wasn't she? When we approach time as a looming creature that takes away moments and takes away opportunity, it narrows our understanding and appreciation of time. If we see moments as ticking away, we are anxious and fearful of all sorts of things slipping away. But when we see time as one fruitful moment of potential after another, it shifts our mindset. Rather than time ticking away, time becomes a series of moments that come upon us, that wash over us. Moments to embrace or not. Moments to seize upon or not. Moments to be present or not. But new moments nonetheless. A new moment that is as fleeting as our last moment.

EMOTION IS MEANT TO MOVE THROUGH US

Take the phrase "to be moved by something;" this adage illustrates the human truth that feelings move through us. Emotions are dynamic. Always moving. Never still. To allow feeling to move through us and shift and change is a profound human experience. To be alive is to understand that nothing within us is truly still.

What does that mean – that something within us is dynamic and that our bodies are never truly still? Do you remember playing freeze tag as a child? Can you recall that distinct feeling of having to hold still until someone tagged you? I don't know about you, but that was a miserable feeling for me; it was awkward and unnatural. Our bodies are meant to move freely. Our lungs breathe. Our muscles contract and release. Our feelings flow freely.

If we hold still, like in freeze tag, tension builds. If I hold my breath, I feel an energy or a tightness build – this holding means that I will eventually need to inhale or gasp for air. When we freeze, we are attempting to do the impossible – to still a moving body.

A bodyworker once told me that my physical body felt frozen, like I had been holding my breath for years. And my body, she remarked, was oddly cold to touch, like a corpse. Yikes! This was ironic, because having lived much of my life as a dancer, I expressed myself through movement and creativity – both vital and dynamic processes. How odd that my muscles and soft tissues had ended up so taut and lifeless? My diaphragm was stiff and held tight. My neck and jaw clenched. My body armor – my armored emotional reality – had become my rigid physical reality, or maybe it was the other way around. I couldn't tell. But one thing was for sure: I wasn't taking full breaths, and I wasn't living a full life.

As a mother, I know firsthand how hard it is to ask a child to sit still. Because they exist entirely in the present moment, young children demonstrate that the body moves when we feel and play. All of our states of being, including sleeping and resting, are embodied with dynamic energy. Our bodies are not stone statues. Even if we hold our bodies still for a short time, the biochemistry of our bodies and cells are humming along. As we stand in stillness, our heart beats, our postural muscles keep us from toppling to the floor, and our neurons fire impulses.

As a bodyworker who uses touch as a therapeutic tool, I'm constantly aware of the different waves and pulses in the body. Whether what

I'm feeling is a breath, a pulse, a craniosacral rhythm, a warmth, or a very palpable energy emanating from a body, our bodies are in constant flux. Our feelings and emotions are just another element of flux, shift, and movement in our lives. To be present with ourselves is to let our feelings move us and exist unimpeded.

By choosing mindfulness over mindlessness, we also accept change and impermanence. In the same manner that our bodies are always moving, life does not stand still and is never frozen in time. Flux and change are inevitable. The impermanent nature of life is all that is guaranteed. What's the saying? "Nothing is certain but death and taxes." And I would add that the earth spins, a new day dawns, and everything can change in a heartbeat.

Embracing the impermanence of life means understanding that we don't, or rather can't, hold on to things, even if we want to. And we certainly can't hold on to feelings. No matter how hard we may try, we can't freeze a moment in time.

Consider these moments that we might wish to hold on to or freeze in time...

- A feeling of accomplishment that fills us with pride or a feeling of being appreciated or loved
- A flush of energy from exercise or a clean bill of health from your doctor
- A brand-new car's shiny and glossy perfection or a clean and organized house

- A moment of quiet
- A feeling of success or happiness

When we have a momentary experience that feels like perfection, we hang on; when we have a momentary feeling that is painful or uncomfortable, we feel stuck in its endless grasp. Grasping and embracing impermanence entails holding two contradictory truths at one time. Not only is it impossible to hang on to a momentary feeling of fabulousness, it is futile and exhausting – a complete waste of your precious energy. Conversely, difficult felt emotion is not endless nor is it frozen in time. Remember, another moment is right around the corner and can bring another, quite different, feeling.

Holding our breath or trying to freeze does not shield us from our present moment – and certainly will not shield us from heartache, breakups, or difficult times. Even if we carefully construct walls and body armor around our heart and emotions, life will keep picking us up, shaking us, and tossing us around – sometimes gently, sometimes mercilessly.

When we fight our own emotions, we are resisting the natural flow of life and consequently taxing our feeling muscle. But when we open to feeling, we align with change and impermanence, because we accept that life is ever-changing, and we effortlessly embrace life's transient nature.

WHAT ABOUT UNFATHOMABLE AND IMMEASURABLE EMOTIONAL PAIN?

If we encourage ourselves to stay with hard feelings, an inevitable question arises — what about emotional pain that does indeed go on and on? We may inherently understand that singular feelings, like embarrassment or frustration, are fleeting, but what about someone experiencing an unfathomable loss or trauma?

Telling someone who has experienced the death of a loved one that their feelings are temporary may sound outrageous and unrealistic at best, or hurtful and insensitive at worst. But we can assure an individual experiencing the deepest pain that what they are feeling in their bodies is valid and that the intensity, shape, and form of their felt emotion will change and shift. While the idea or thought of their loss may feel unending, felt emotion will invariably change its shape.

We have all heard the phrase "get to the other side of grief." What does that mean to someone so heartbroken and devastated by their emotional pain? In response to incomprehensible and immeasurable pain, I use the analogy of two sides of the same coin to describe how our feelings can take different shapes. Imagine that the loss of a loved one is the coin; the coin is always there, but the sides of the coin can change and flip. One side may be an unending, cavernous hole in our heart, while another side may be a glorious memory or a feeling of the truest and purest love you could ever imagine.

When we use the expression "get to other side of a feeling," we are acknowledging and accepting that we are capable of feeling other feelings. A different feeling. A new feeling. Maybe a ridiculously fleeting feeling, but we can move through to another feeling. Remember, in acute grief and trauma, this may sound absurd or even cruel to someone; for someone bearing an unimaginable feeling, another side to the coin may feel impossible. Our timetables are all different.

Getting through a feeling simply means moving to the possibility of another feeling. And of course, there are not only two sides (or two feelings) to deep trauma and emotional pain; rather there are many, many, many sides – and many, many, many feelings. When a painful emotion feels like it will never end, it may be helpful to remember that another emotion might be just around the corner. And that not all feelings will be as hard.

Paradoxically, there may be instances where someone does not want a heartache or loss to end. At first glance, this may seem perplexing; however, as we look deeper, it simply reflects another side, or another beautiful nuance, to our proverbial coin. I recently bumped into Faith, a colleague and fellow Frequent Feeler, and in our catching up, Faith shared with me her very raw experience with grief – the recent loss of her beloved dog Lily. It had been less than a year since Faith and her husband had had to euthanize Lily, and it was a heart- and gut-wrenching decision that had brought them both to their knees.

Faith explained to me that Lily had been her baby. Lily had opened Faith's heart and enabled her to feel loved in a way that no human relationship had before. For months after Lily passed, Faith felt a mixture of profound guilt, regret, sadness, yearning, and confusion. So many emotions collided to shape Faith's complex experience of Lily's loss, as she shared, "I recognized how deeply I loved her by how deeply I grieved."

What Faith said next shed light on how intricate and elegant our emotions can be. "In the midst of my grieving, I felt a secondary grief around the grief ending because I didn't want that profound love for her to fade." Faith explained to me that she mourned "the loss of grief," because she knew her feelings would eventually recede. The realization that her sorrow and heartache would, in time, move on broke Faith's heart.

Impossible feelings can feel like there is no end in sight, and yet sometimes our impossible feelings are the only thing that connect us to what is real and all-encompassing in our lives. Sometimes, everything else going on in our lives can feel trivial compared to the deep feelings that exist within us. Whether our emotions are brief houseguests, whether they overstay their welcome, or whether the length of their visit feels just right, feelings do connect us to the experiences that make our hearts beat and our hearts break. When we feel strongly and profoundly, it can be a reflection of how much we have been touched or moved or loved. And sometimes our emotions are exactly where we want to be.

CHAPTER SIX EXPERIENTIAL

I. BODY PLAY: FIND AN ECHO IN YOUR BODY

Let's play with the idea of creating energy and sensation in the body that reverberates through us. This energy can help us feel ourselves and reminds us that we do exist in a physical form. We are not just ideas, thoughts, and words. We have a depth and a density.

- Start standing, if you are able, with a bit of space around you to move. Begin GENTLY bouncing, swaying, jiggling, or shaking your whole body (or just a single body part). Please be mindful of any movement that might hurt or aggravate an existing injury or condition; this exercise can be done in a very gentle manner and can be modified. As you move your body in this bouncy or jiggly way, you may begin to feel sensations, energy, and possibly a weight to parts of your body. Let these feelings build within you.

- After roughly three to five minutes of moving your body. Pause the movement. Allow the movement to find an echo in your body, where you feel the energy, sensation, or awakening still within you. Allow this echo to continue as you stand still and then as you move into the continuation of your day.

2. A SIMPLE AWARENESS: WHERE DOES YOUR ATTENTION GO?

Spend five to ten minutes noticing where your attention goes. Remember that where your attention goes is where you spend your time and energy, so to speak. This exercise is simply for you to begin to notice to where and to what your attention goes within a short period of time. Is your attention busy, shifting from one thing to the next? Are you ruminating on a single thought or feeling? Are you staying focused on one thing? Remember, there is no right or wrong, only neutral observation.

Sit in a comfortable position and take a moment to feel your inhale and exhale. Welcome in your Neutral Observer and release any judgment, criticism, or agenda that you might have. With a neutral and accepting attitude, simply notice the things that your attention is drawn to. For example, your attention may start with a worry or a nagging thought, it might move to how hungry you are and then move to the dishes that need to be washed. Resist attaching to any single thought or worry or feeling. For five to ten minutes, simply observe where your attention is and what it moves to next. That's all.

EXPERIENTIAL

3. "ASK YOURSELF SOME QUESTIONS" PROMPT

You will notice that the section "Does This Behavior Move You Toward or Away from Yourself? And What Does That Mean?" has quite a few questions. There is a lot to sink your teeth into as you look back at the bulleted questions in that section.

Consider choosing one or more questions to reflect on and answer. Find a question that piques your interest: meditate on it, write about it, or deeply feel and sit with it. The intention is for you to identify your goals and desires in life and to begin to see how certain choices and behaviors bring you closer to yourself, your goals, your loved ones, and the present moment... or possibly further away. Remember to enlist your Neutral Observer.

EXPERIENTIAL

CHAPTER SEVEN

RIDING THE WAVE
OF EMOTION

*Something had to give. I knew that I no longer wanted to live
a numb and isolated life. I wanted connection. And I wanted
to be present and engaged in my life. I couldn't be afraid
of feeling the messiness and the discomfort of living. For if
I numbed myself from the messiness, I invariably numbed
myself from the things in my life that were meaningful and
wonderful. I needed to prove to myself that I could get
to the other side of hard feelings and hard situations. To
outlast the discomfort, I had to learn to ride my feelings.*

FELT EMOTIONS ARE WAVES

Felt emotion has a beginning, a middle, and an end. The duration is variable but be assured that an end is in sight. We tend to forget this, and rather than riding the wave, we block it, stop it, or avoid it.

Take a moment and recall the last time you felt sadness. Maybe you wept or shed a single tear. Maybe your sadness was felt — perhaps a burrowing hole in your gut, a weight on your heart, a heaviness behind your eyes. There may have been a moment in your experience of sadness, whatever that was for you, when you wondered, will this feeling ever end, will this heaviness ever subside, will this gut-wrenching pain ever pass? Did it? Has it?

Think about the last time you got angry. Did you allow yourself to ride the anger? Did you allow the feeling to fill you, to crescendo and then to dissipate? Or did you hold it in, swallow it, or spew it out explosively?

Emotions are indeed waves. And they behave like them in every way. Some waves are small and gentle. Some are enormous and rolling. Some kiss the shore gently, and some erode the sand with their rapid strength. No matter the intensity, emotions ebb and flow.

While obvious in hindsight, in the throes of tough emotion, it is very hard to see and believe our emotions' wavelike pattern. Emotion can feel unending and unrelenting when we are being tossed around by its wave; the transient nature of emotion is so very hard to embrace when an end is not in sight. We can indeed learn and trust that emotions are fluid and impermanent, yet this is not an easy task.

THE ONLY WAY IS THROUGH: RIDING THE WAVE

Our only hope in staying with and outlasting difficult felt emotion is to ride its wave. Imagine for a moment, the feeling of bodysurfing a wave. I had the enviable experience of growing up on Nantucket Island. I was surrounded by waves. Yes, waves in every direction. To the north, south, east, and west. Trust me, I know of what I speak – I know the feeling of riding waves, both literally and figuratively.

It can be scary. It can be lovely and gentle. It can be invigorating. It can be tumultuous. It can be peaceful. When you're out in the Nantucket surf, no matter what the wave looks like, it is coming right at you. You dive through it. You jump over it. You let it take you up and over the swell. But you can't duck it or swerve it. The only way is through. The same goes for felt emotion – the only way is through.

While writing this book, I had an example of riding the wave of emotional discomfort, or rather not riding the wave, stare me right in the face. Even though I had accompanied my patients as they rode many waves of challenging feelings, I couldn't see something that was so very close to me. Instead, it snuck up on me and surprised me.

While in the process of writing *The Feeling Muscle*, a loved one, whom I will call Jim, was struggling with and receiving treatment for

OCD (obsessive-compulsive disorder). OCD manifested in Jim as a need to repeat behaviors over and over again until he had an inside feeling that he had done the behavior "just right." For example, he might need to touch an object again and again until something inside himself gave him a green light. Then, and only then, could he move forward with his day.

Jim was undergoing Exposure and Response Prevention (ERP) therapy, where he was actively and intentionally disengaging from his repeating behaviors. This therapy was bringing up significant anxiety for him. One day, while I was sitting in on one of Jim's therapy sessions, his psychologist drew a bell curve (a wave!) on a whiteboard in his office; this bell curve was to illustrate what Jim needed to do to fight his OCD. As his doctor explained, Jim needed to outlast his wave of anxiety from start to finish. And if he could do that, Jim's OCD would lose its power, and he could regain some control over his life.

Let me try to explain it a bit better, as OCD, if you are not familiar with it, is complex and difficult to grasp. Jim's brain was telling him that he had to engage in rituals and compulsions (remember, our brain can tell us many things that are untrue); if he did not engage, he got "a feeling" that something very bad was going to happen, an intense anxiety that was unbearable to his core. Conversely, when he listened to and obeyed his OCD, meaning he engaged in his ritual or compulsion, his anxiety would go away. In essence, his rituals brought him relief from his anxiety.

His psychologist explained that to fully ride out his anxiety, Jim would need to tolerate the whole bell curve of his anxiety, as it started, crested, lessened, and then eventually dissipated. Yes, if he could tolerate and outlast his anxiety, he would begin to realize – and more importantly, trust – that the wave of his anxiety would eventually end. In due course, Jim could refrain from his ritual, outlast his anxiety, and gather the inner data that something bad did not happen as a result.

While Jim's psychologist did not talk specifically about the body's experience (Jim's felt emotion) during the curve and rather talked more cognitively and abstractly about Jim's ability to "tolerate the discomfort of his anxiety," I knew immediately that he was asking Jim to ride the wave of his felt anxiety. Jim felt things strongly in his body, and he needed to learn to tolerate his felt inner discomfort. This was key to the treatment of Jim's OCD.

INTERFERING WITH THE WAVE:
STOPPING VS. FREEZING

Just like waves in the ocean are different in size, strength, and intensity, the waves of our felt emotion follow suit. But unlike an ocean wave, we can, with the help of our judgment, desires, and critical thought, get in the way of our felt emotion. Sometimes we want to stop it and push it away and, conversely, sometimes we try to freeze it and keep it forever.

Remember our society's and our caregivers' messages – the messages that certain emotions should be controlled or swallowed.

Well, when we heed these messages, we interfere with the wave. If we get the message as young children that showing emotions is a punishable or intolerable act, we may consequently shut down our emotions. We stunt the natural wave dynamic of felt emotion.

Conversely, we often get a different message when we feel and express our joy, happiness, and contentment. These emotions are allowed to flow more freely and, at times, are even praised and rewarded by the world around us. And you know what, they feel better too. I'd prefer to feel contentment over fear any day. In these instances, if we say yes to the pleasurable feelings, we say to the wave, "Come on in," as it crescendos and wanes, no problem. We don't get in its way. Or do we?

An interesting observation that I made working with patients on my table is that we can interfere with all our feelings, whether they feel good or not. It may be understandable that we swallow and push away dread or guilt as those emotions aren't all that fun to feel. But why mess around with trust or hope, as they are such delightful feelings to be a part of?

Have you ever had a feeling that was so lovely, exciting, and warm that you didn't want it to end? "If only I could hold onto this feeling" is an idiom we use in the English language; the phrase aptly describes how, if we could, we would freeze our wonderful and lovely feelings and capture them in time. When we are experiencing a euphoric or intensely happy, joyful, or fulfilling emotion, we may have a fervent desire to hang onto or freeze that feeling — to keep it. Just as we may push a dreadful feeling away, we can approach the fleeting nature of a lovely feeling with apprehension or even muscular tension, as we are trying to do the impossible — to catch a wave, hold on to it, or freeze it for eternity.

To the contrary, when we experience strong and profound feelings of sadness, grief, guilt, or despair, we have a very difficult time trusting that the feelings will end. In a moment, we will read about Ellen. Ellen had an intense fear that if she let herself weep, she would never stop. This fear is not unique to Ellen. In fact, I have had many patients on my table who were convinced a difficult feeling would consume them and never go away. This fear can keep patients from touching or revisiting deep feelings buried within.

Ellen told me that she was afraid that she "would not survive" her feeling of great sadness. Before we chalk this up to hyperbole, we might look to references in literature where characters are overtaken by or even perish of a broken heart. While not aligned with an understanding of modern medicine, the idea of succumbing to strong emotion reinforces how strongly emotions are felt and even how dangerous or deadly they can feel within us. If we note that Shakespeare attributes both King Lear's and Romeo and Juliet's Lady Montague's death to grief, perhaps it's not completely out of the realm of possibility that a person may fear succumbing to or perishing from a painful or devastating emotion.

How strange it is that we believe or fear some emotions will never end, while we know from our own experience that other much more favorable emotions are fleeting. But the end result is the same — whether we embrace and covet certain emotions or whether we go to great lengths to not feel others, we are still in the habit of interfering with them.

ELLEN: I'M AFRAID I WON'T SURVIVE THE FEELING

Ellen came to a session one day feeling especially vulnerable. Her emotions were at the surface, based on a recent argument she had had with her husband. When she came into my office, I could tell she was rattled.

Ellen and I had worked together for many years. She had first come to me for nutritional counseling after revealing to her therapist a long history of disordered eating. For fifteen years she had alternated between binge and restrictive eating patterns. Our early doctor-patient relationship had remained at the nutritional level, so to speak, but had gradually evolved over time to a deeper exploration of the mind-body connection. As our therapeutic relationship progressed, Ellen shared more about her work with her therapist and was interested in exploring her relationship with and to her body — as years of an undiagnosed eating disorder had left her with a critical and even combative partnership with her body.

On this particular day, Ellen asked to go right to the table and skip the roughly ten minutes of checking in we would normally do. She was restless in both her body and mind, and she wanted to find that quieter place that she thought she could find on the table.

When Ellen lay down on my bodywork table, I could tell that she was "trying" to relax. If you have tried to relax when you are hyped up emotionally, you know it is a tall order. In fact, I intentionally present the concept of relaxing to patients as not something we "do," but rather a state of being. While relaxation techniques are important skills to have and are part of the mind-body toolkit, accepting where we are in any given moment is key to being and staying in the present. For Ellen, trying to relax on this particular day was futile.

I gently put my hands on her shoulders and encouraged her to have no agenda on the table. I guided Ellen with my words: "Try to resist changing the present moment in any way. Accept where you are in this moment, whatever that may bring."

"I feel empty," Ellen said with a combination of sadness and agitation. We both let those words settle in the silence that followed. After a few minutes, I repeated her words, "You feel empty."

Ellen placed her left hand over her solar plexus – just below the ribcage but above her belly button. "I feel empty here," she went on. "As if I have been punched in the gut, and what is left is a hole. A gaping hole."

When I asked Ellen if she was able to stay with that feeling for a bit, she reported that the emptiness was painful to feel and hard for her to stay with. She told me with both strain and fear in her voice that this feeling was familiar to her. She knew the feeling, and she had felt it at different times in her life. She admitted that she had never stayed with it long enough to get to know the feeling or what might happen if she did.

I could see Ellen pull away from the feeling as she started to tell me what had happened earlier that day. She began to describe how her husband had become intensely angry with her while having an argument over their finances. "I know he won't, but a part of me is afraid he might leave me," Ellen said in a frightened hush. I validated Ellen's feelings, "You are feeling fear right now."

I noted in my mind that Ellen's fear of abandonment was possibly triggering this familiar feeling for her, as she admitted she had felt this "gaping hole" at other times in her life. For a moment I was tempted to ask Ellen more about the argument and whether she had felt a similar fear of someone leaving in her past, but I knew that would take her away from the feeling and back into her thoughts.

Both Ellen's moving away from the feeling by verbally describing the argument and my temptation to ask more questions are illustrations of how our default is often to get wrapped up in narratives. Again, narratives can be helpful and offer constructive reflection and awareness of ourselves; however, we are accustomed to going to our minds rather than our bodies for insight. I had to silently remind myself (even as a bodyworker and feeler), "Resist the urge to talk more and stay with Ellen's empty feeling in her gut."

I gently encouraged Ellen to stay with her body and her feeling. I gently put my hands over her hand that rested upon her upper abdomen. I asked her to stay with the feeling if she could, and reminded her, kindly and gently, to do so without judgment or agenda.

After many minutes of silence, Ellen told me that she felt like she needed to cry. "Not just cry," she told me. "I need to weep."

I reassured her that I was there with her in that moment. We had a solid therapeutic relationship from working together for many years, where she trusted that I could hold space for her emotions. She knew that I had no set expectations of her, and that the four walls of my office were a safe space for her to feel.

What she said next surprised me. And her words would be echoed by other patients on my table in the years to come.

"But I can't cry," she said and then paused. "Because if I do, I will never stop." She paused again. "I'm afraid I won't survive the feeling. The sadness is too great." We stayed quietly together, my hand on her hand, in the moments that followed.

It was a big deal for Ellen to be able to stay with her "empty" feeling that session. I have learned as a bodyworker and as a shepherd of feelings that, first and foremost, we need to honor our feelings. We can offer someone the space to feel, and we can build a mutual trust that feelings will be held in that space with great care and respect, but feelings cannot be forced. They cannot be pried open or prematurely drawn out.

In that moment, I held space for Ellen's truth — the truth that she believed that she would not survive her sadness. I did not say, "Oh, sure you can handle it." I did not say, "Of course you will survive it." Instead, we both sat with her words and her truth — the fact that if she let herself cry, she would never stop and perhaps not survive. Her sadness felt too all-encompassing, too dangerous to feel, and that was what she needed to acknowledge in that moment.

PULL YOURSELF TOGETHER
AND PUT A LID ON IT

The idea of holding emotions in and not letting them out is part of our consciousness, as evidenced by everyday language. It is not as if the concept of bottling up our feelings is unknown to us. Right? Consider all the expressions for keeping our emotions in check…

- You may be called a closed book, thick-skinned, unruffled, bottled up, stone-faced, cold and detached.
- You may be told to buckle down, grit your teeth, collect yourself, hold back tears, put on a brave face, suffer in silence, keep a stiff upper lip, put a lid on it, grow tougher skin, get over it, don't wear your emotions on your sleeve, pull yourself together.
- You may have internalized statements like "this is not the place for that" or "boys don't cry."

If we reread these words along with the idea of emotions being wavelike and dynamic, don't these phrases all imply the opposite – a holding in or a holding back of energy? These words suggest that controlling our emotions involves effort to contain or immobilize something that should flow.

I would posit that the words we choose to express, both showing emotion and not showing emotion, offer an implicit understanding that emotions are meant to move through us and move through our bodies; inherently we understand that emotions are dynamic and fluid, and that it involves effort, in some form or another, to hold them back or resist the wave.

When we apply this idea to felt emotion, we can assume that holding in our feelings would involve muscular or energetic tension within the body. It would strain our feeling muscle. This makes sense when we acknowledge that body armor is a real phenomenon and that it is exhausting to interfere with or hold unfelt or stagnant emotion within us.

OPENING THE EMOTIONAL FLOODGATES

When we use tension in the body to block, numb, and swallow our feelings (feelings that are meant to move through us), we are essentially building a dam within us. Hence, the commonly used phrase "opening the floodgates" when referring to an emotional release.

When working with patients, I often use guided imagery to help patients experience certain feelings or concepts within the body. Consider these two very different images:

- INTERFERING WITH THE WAVE: I regularly use the example of "trying to move forward with the parking brake on" to describe how we get in the way of our emotions. Take a moment and feel what it would be like to walk or run forward with the parking brake on. You most likely can relate to the stunted and effortful nature of that feeling. When we get in the way of the wave of emotion, we are using effort, at times exhaustively, to halt a natural, dynamic process. This effort is evident in phrases like "swallowing anger" and "holding back tears."

- RIDING THE WAVE: Now for a totally different inner experience, imagine riding a wave. From the moment you catch the swell of the wave to when you arrive at the point where the wave leaves you, let the wave carry you. Surrender, so to speak, to where the wave takes you. Let go of a need for control and trust that the wave will carry you safely through the up and down or side to side. It feels very different to ride a wave than to stop it or interfere with it. Yes?

Take note of these two very different inner experiences, for I will ask you to recall these feelings later in the book.

One day, while having coffee with a friend, Debra, she shared an experience she had had. Knowing I was a "feelings" person, Debra wanted to tell me about her unexpected reaction while attending a recent funeral. With concern in her voice, she said, "I cried the entire funeral, from the beginning to the end. Like for an hour, I couldn't stop." Debra continued, "It was totally unacceptable, completely unacceptable!"

I don't think Debra's experience is particularly unique. Our emotions can surprise us when they pour out of us and when we realize that we don't have the control over them that we usually do or that we thought we did. Grief is tricky that way, because it can be so powerful and undulating. When you combine the desire to hold back feelings of grief with the overwhelming forcefulness of grief, there is often an inner struggle to try to control or hold it back. You will either win or lose that struggle depending on the day. Debra lost the struggle that day.

Notice Debra's comments on how "unacceptable" her crying was. It went on "like for an hour." Whether or not we think crying at a funeral is acceptable, it can certainly be uncomfortable and awkward, especially if we feel some embarrassment or shame around crying. Debra may have been judging herself for openly expressing her sadness and grief in public. Or maybe she felt it was unacceptable to cry for so long – an hour. We usually have lots of feelings around feeling in public places.

Debra moved on to another subject very quickly and left her "unacceptable" emotional experience behind her. Had I sensed that she wanted to talk more about it, I would have asked her if she would have felt differently had she cried in private for an hour. Our willingness to feel and express emotion can understandably be very different in private than in public. Often, when our emotion threatens to overflow in public, we employ herculean efforts to push it down.

During my grandmother's funeral, my nineteen-year-old self, with little insight into my emotional self, sat tense and frozen, alternating yawns and swallows to try to keep my floodgates from opening. Lots of yawns and lots of swallows. Looking around me, I saw such stoic faces, and I followed suit, putting on a stiff upper lip and placing a heavy stone lid on the powerful boiling of sadness within me.

I sat at my grandmother's funeral alone, despite the fact that there were dozens of people around me. I sat alone in my feelings, overwhelmed by all the feeling inside that had nowhere to go.

With each yawn and each swallow, I added brick upon brick to my emotional dam.

Does the idea of an emotional dam resonate? Emotional dams are built...

- When we hold feelings in. When we don't want to express our feelings. Or don't know how.
- When we feel confusion, embarrassment, or shame around our feelings.
- When we expect our feelings to be belittled or berated. When we don't feel safe showing our feelings.
- When we believe that no one will understand our feelings. When we think we are the only ones with these feelings.

When we look at Debra's experience at the funeral, we see that what she considered to be socially unacceptable kept her from fully validating her emotions. Her emotions were so great and powerful that she could not swallow or stop them, but she could still manage to judge herself. Debra's Inner Critic was hard at work during the funeral saying, "This is not okay. Put a lid on it."

Debra did not want to ride her wave of grief that day. Or didn't want to in public. Or didn't know how. All these struggles are valid. I don't know whether she was in the habit of riding her emotional waves in private, but she was powerless in her efforts to shut them off in that moment.

Some of us may recognize a moment like Debra's struggle to keep the floodgates from opening in our own lives, when we were incapable of closing off or pushing down an emotion. The floodgates opened, and we were powerless to manage the flow; our emotion came out regardless of any effort to the contrary.

Were we to have more experience with riding our emotional waves growing up, I posit that we might not need or experience floodgates opening unexpectedly. We might not build the dam within ourselves that grows so tall and so wide and so strong. That dam — that separates us from our emotions and creates a pressure variance in our bodies — would be unnecessary as we would feel our emotions freely as they came up and avoid an emotional backup.

BODY BREAK

Take a moment and close your eyes. Imagine you just pulled the parking brake to your body. Resist questioning what the heck that means. Simply try to imagine it and feel it – whatever it means to you. After a minute or two, shift to a completely new image, and visualize that you are riding a wave, surrendering to the wave. Allow it to carry you. Resist any desire to control where or how the wave carries you. Practice surrendering to the ride. That's all.

WHEN NOTHING GETS THROUGH: AN OVERFORTIFIED EMOTIONAL DAM

When we build an emotional dam, we run the risk of blocking more than just the feelings we don't want to feel. Occasionally our dam is so well fortified by our body armor and our habits of stuffing and burying feelings that very few feelings, if any, get through.

Feelings of joy, amusement, love, and contentment – feelings that we would otherwise bask in and enjoy – are met with the same rocklike barrier that fights to keep hard feelings away. Our feeling muscle works overtime, coming up against our dam again and again. Sometimes, our feeling muscle just gives up. As a result, we are numb to feelings that would be very lovely to feel.

I remember the summer after I graduated from naturopathic medical school, when I spent months studying, day in and day out, for my licensing board exams. My habit of running from feelings combined with my depletion from years of schooling and my intense trepidation of the pending exams created a perfect storm within me. My emotions were held so tight, and I felt especially numb. It didn't matter if feelings were joyful or scary, or hopeful or painful; I didn't feel them. When our emotional dam looms so large, even pleasure and mirth can't find their way through.

When I consciously made a commitment to feeling again, it was like getting back on my feet after a long illness. My dam was stubborn because it had become part of my inner makeup for so long. It took time, and it took a willingness to feel all types of feelings. It began with very small waves making their way through — small glimmers of hope and excitement, frustration and regret.

Luckily, my smaller waves gave way to waves of different sizes and strengths. As my dam became more pliable and porous, more emotions began to peek through and then break through. Because I held back feeling for so long, emotion would pop up erratically and with surprising strength and power.

At times, my floodgates would tear open with emotion that surprised and scared me. My heart and my head would pulse with undulating sadness. My chest, arms, and hands would ache and pound with powerful anger. My soul would twist and turn as unrelenting and towering fear tossed around inside of me. It felt so raw, so foreign, and so new.

It took time to begin to unpack and manage all that I felt inside of me. My feeling muscle was relaxing and releasing bit by bit. My surprise at my floodgates opening demonstrates how emotions can feel unpredictable, especially when we are so used to holding them in. They can pour out unexpectedly and unceremoniously. Emotions catch us off guard. I remember being confused about how my sadness sometimes came out as frustration, or my tears as laughter. Remarkably, my feelings of appreciation, gratitude, and elation were much more pronounced. Setting my feelings free meant feeling hard stuff, but it made the great stuff come alive in me in bigger and more beautiful ways.

My joy would fill me from the belly up. My laughter would travel through my whole body, from my toes to the crown of my head. Passion was palpable within me. Appreciation would surround and overflow from my heart. Excitement and delight would dance within me.

Floodgates open in different ways in different people. Not all of us cry; not all of us weep or wail or scream. Grief and sadness do not always open into tears; rage, anger, hate, and frustration can emerge. The body can boil with sadness, pulse with grief, and break open with loss. Our hearts can hurt, our heads can ache, and our guts can wrench with different emotions. Our emotional experiences are vast and unique. Each of us has our own distinctive emotional path to forge, and if we can open ourselves to the process, some pretty cool feelings may find us too.

DON'T BE SURPRISED IF EMOTIONS SHAPESHIFT

While shapeshifting – the ability to change state, form, or appearance – is common in science fiction movies and Greek mythology, it is a real phenomenon when it comes to felt emotion. When you get in the habit of sitting with feelings, you will notice that one of two things can happen – the feeling you are sitting with will either eventually fade away, or it can change shape.

What do I mean by change shape? By now, we understand that felt emotion is a tangible inner experience. Felt emotion takes shape within us – it has a location, a density, and an intensity. After sitting with a particular feeling, we may notice that the feeling shifts to a new location or perhaps has taken on a different shape altogether. Sometimes before a feeling has fully run its course, it becomes a totally new feeling. And occasionally a feeling lingers within us longer than usual.

Years back, I was working with Connor on my bodywork table. He was staying with a very intense bubbling feeling in his chest. Connor was going through a divorce and was processing feelings of anger, powerlessness, and loss. He was surprised when the intense feeling in his chest moved, rather suddenly, to his abdomen. This new feeling in his abdomen was different and denser than the bubbling in his chest; it had weight and more substance to it. I remember Connor called the density "a sad heaviness." This heavy weight was bringing home the significant loss he was feeling in his life.

In this example, Connor's commitment to stay with a feeling did not bring a resolution; instead, it brought a different feeling for him to feel. While I'd like to be able to say that all feelings resolve or dissipate, the reality is that some simply change shape. Indeed, it can be frustrating when we begin to pay attention to a feeling, only to find that a new one pops up in its place – or in a different place. This new feeling may be a completely different feeling, or it may be a new iteration of the original feeling.

Be assured, however, that when a feeling changes shape, it is still dynamic and wavelike. When emotions shapeshift, it does not mean that you have blocked or interfered with the feeling; rather, you have stayed with the feeling long enough for it to do what it needs to do. And some feelings need to change shape before they run their course.

You may or may not have the time or energy to stay with the shift, but have confidence that you have done good, hard work. You have stayed with a feeling long enough to set it free — and that freedom allows it to move, breathe, and change shape within you.

TUNING INTO THE BODY
VS. HYPERFOCUSING ON FEELINGS

A trap that we can fall into when we begin to pay attention to our body's inner experience is that we can become obsessive about or hyperfocused on our bodily sensations. In a similar way that we ruminate upon thoughts, concerns, and stresses in our lives, we can ruminate about sensations or feelings within our bodies.

You may be, quite possibly, throwing up your hands with exasperation and saying to yourself, but isn't that what this book is about? Isn't being hyperfocused on our body's feelings what this book is advocating for? No, it's not.

There is a significant difference between observing, sitting with, and outlasting our body's feelings — and hyperfocusing on them. Frequent Feelers, and even folks who are not feelers, can become fixated on feelings occurring in the body when asked to focus on them, and just like we can perseverate on a thought or a worry, we can obsess about feelings in the body.

- Does this feeling mean I have an illness?
- Is something wrong with my body?
- Am I about to have a panic attack?

Bringing our attention and awareness to the body can ramp up some of our worries and concerns about our health; for some, bringing awareness to our bodies can exacerbate a tendency to hyperfocus on a singular aspect of ourselves, like tension in the jaw, discomfort in the hips, or a jitteriness in the chest. And in doing so, we can convince ourselves that something is amiss.

As I mentioned in Chapter One, the more we get to know our felt emotion — our usual suspects — the better we will know when a new feeling warrants a call to the doctor. We will know when a feeling does not pass or dissipate or shapeshift, and we will act accordingly. But becoming acquainted with our feelings does not mean hyperfocusing on them. Remember the dynamic and wavelike nature of emotion. Feelings are meant to be felt, not obsessed over.

As we become better acquainted with our feelings, we actually become better friends with our bodies. We let go of having a combative, fearful, or high-alert relationship with our bodies and forge a healthier and more connected one. As we gain trust, understanding, and acceptance of our feelings, we embrace and nurture a neutral and attuned relationship with our bodies.

LET'S PLAY IN THE WAVES

It's not unusual for me to give patients homework. When someone is starting to explore deeper parts of themselves, a daily commitment to some kind of exercise, visualization, meditation, or journaling practice keeps them focused on and dedicated to their process. In fact, the experiential sections at the end of each chapter reflect many of the homework assignments I give my patients.

You may have noticed that I call some of the experiential exercises "Body Play." When giving homework to my patients, I will often use the word "play" as my preferred verb.

- Play with this meditation or visualization
- Play with this new concept in your life
- Play with the idea of staying present while you are...

Patients sometimes comment on how much they like the term "play" because it makes the ideas more relatable and approachable. Mind-body concepts and techniques challenge the way we think and behave – and that can be hard. Nonetheless, if they can be approached with curiosity, vulnerability, and an attitude of playfulness, we can begin to trust that a new or different way of doing something is possible.

When we challenge longstanding and entrenched beliefs about how we have operated in the world, we might get our guard up and go on the defensive. But we don't have to approach new ideas with defensive postures. We can take them slowly. We can "play" with the ideas. Playing with the possibility of doing something differently takes the sting out of the process. It allows us to let our guard down and relax our prickly defenses, resulting in the trust required to let something new in.

Let's play in the waves.

CHAPTER SEVEN EXPERIENTIAL

I. BODY PLAY: "BREATH IS A WAVE" MEDITATION

You may want to record your voice reading this guided imagery script to play back while you are quietly and comfortably resting or meditating. Or simply read the script first and meditate on the words, concepts, or images.

Begin by finding a comfortable position: sitting, lying on the floor or a mat, or resting in a supported manner. Your eyes may be open or closed. Take a few moments to feel your body. Scan your body from head to toe to notice any areas of tension, gripping, or holding. Bring the idea of ease into your body – whatever that means to you.

Visualize that you are on a beach or somewhere near the sea. You are comfortable. Warm. At ease. You are facing the ocean and simply noticing each wave as it washes onto shore. Notice that each wave is different. Different strengths. Different swells. Some waves just barely creep up the shore. Some waves roll in with powerful rumbles. Some waves kiss your feet as you sit watching. Continue to visualize different waves as they roll ashore. Gently and with intention, shift your visualization from watching the waves to simply noticing your breath. Rather than observing ocean waves, observe each inhale and exhale. Let go of any preconceived notion that there is a right or wrong way to breathe. You are breathing exactly as you should.

*Begin to observe your breath in the same manner that
you observed each wave – as if each inhale is the wave
rolling on to shore and the exhale is the wave rolling back
to sea. Bring the same level of observation to each breath.
You noticed each wave at a distance; you had no control
over the strength, power, or surge of each wave. OBSERVE
YOUR BREATH WITH A SIMILAR DISTANCE. Avoid trying to
control or change your breath in any way; remember you
can't control or change waves in the ocean. Allow each
breath to be a wave that you simply observe. Stay with
observing your breath for five to ten minutes.*

2. A FELT EMOTION VISUALIZATION

The intention behind this visualization is to envision a situation
(real or imagined) where you anticipate feelings of strong
emotion. You will want to decide on a situation prior to
beginning this exercise so you can dive right into the process.
Perhaps you may visualize a difficult or dreaded conversation,
an awkward or foreboding event, or an anxiety-provoking
situation. You will imagine the situation with great detail so that
you experience the felt emotion it generates, as if the situation
were happening in real time. You will then practice exploring
and getting acquainted with your felt emotion.

*Find a comfortable position and take a few minutes to
quiet your thoughts and feel your body. Begin to visualize*

a situation that you anticipate will generate strong emotion within you. Visualize it in great detail to bring about a feeling. Keep your focus on the body and explore any physical, tangible sensations that come up within you.

Resist the urge to "try" or "force" a feeling to surface within you; you can always try this exercise again at a different time if no felt emotion emerges. If you find yourself going up into your head with thoughts, agendas, or judgments, softly and kindly bring your attention back to the body. Allow this to be time you spend in your body, not your mind. Where is the feeling within you? Does the feeling have a shape, a density, an intensity? Can you stay with the feeling for a while? Get to know your felt emotion.

3. "A TIME WHEN I..." PROMPT

Choose one or both statements below as a springboard for a journal entry, a painting, a meditation, a poem, a song, a dance, or any form of creative expression. Try to recall a time when you either interfered with your emotions or did not have the ability to control them. Remember to be descriptive. Go deep and be honest with yourself.

A time when I bottled up my emotions was...

A time when my floodgates opened and my emotions poured out of me was...

CHAPTER EIGHT

WELCOMING IN FEELING

It took a stark realization to accept that the only way back to living a life complete with meaning, connection, and vitality was for me to have the courage to feel again. My numb and deadened body somehow understood that it needed to learn how to welcome back feeling. And if I could somehow manage to bring back some feeling, I would then need to learn what I never learned to do as a child, adolescent, or young adult — which is to stay with my feelings, to ride out the powerful, sometimes painful feelings, and to learn that I can survive them. And so, while I had spent much of my adolescence and early adulthood braced against, numbing, and running from feeling, I have spent the years since committed to feeling again.

TO FEEL OR NOT TO FEEL

Let's imagine for a moment that we had an "Emotions Class" in elementary school. We have this class just like we have math or gym class. In the first few weeks, we identify all the types of feelings we can have, like joy, fear, happiness, dread, grief, love, acceptance, amusement, anger, rejection, contentment, embarrassment, excitement, shame, and more. We are taught that emotions are waves and that they come and go, ebb and flow. We understand that we can feel multiple emotions at one time, and that they can shapeshift within us. We learn that we feel emotions in our bodies. We learn about felt emotion and our feeling muscle.

We learn that we interfere with our emotions, and that interference can be super helpful to us because it helps us know which emotions are socially acceptable and which are not. And yet, at the same time, we learn that we can influence our emotions with judgment and criticism. We begin to understand that we can shut our feelings down and swallow them.

We role-play to learn by example. We learn that when we act on our anger by kicking our friend, this is not acceptable. Yet we also learn that feeling our anger is normal and valid. We practice talking about our emotions. And we practice feeling them. We understand that emotion is part of being human.

We refrain from judging our emotions as good or bad, but we do acknowledge that some feelings feel better than others. We practice taking in all the warm and joyous feelings with an open heart. We practice staying with yucky feelings. We cheer on our friends as they stay with tough feelings. We feel proud of ourselves when we outlast a hard emotion.

Our class mantras are "the only way is through" and "ride the wave." We learn through each other that we can withstand emotional discomfort and get to the other side. We see how helpful it is to have support and guidance. And we realize it is okay to ask for help. Through real-life experience, we ride the waves of our felt emotion. We begin to gain lived experience – inner data – that we can survive our hard feelings. Our feeling muscle is exercised and cared for.

We celebrate the idea that feelings are like the weather. Some days it will rain. Some days will be sunny. And there will be wind, snow, and hail too.

- What if we had had this class as a child?
- What if we knew and trusted that our rainy days would pass, if only we could wait out the storm?
- What if we were able to resist societal messages, like our storms are too powerful, we really should never storm at all, or we should only drizzle (and in private)?
- What if we grew up with the expectation that we would feel differently on different days? And that we can outlast and survive our storms?

WELCOME-ING IN FEELING

Unfortunately, this Emotions Class doesn't exist in our reality. It didn't, and it doesn't yet. Maybe it will one day. We really are doing so much better with our young children today, as emotional intelligence and emotional wellness are indeed part of the consciousness and even curricula in today's schools. Nevertheless, for so many of us who did not have an emotional education, so to speak, we are left to learn or relearn how to welcome in and stay with emotions on our own.

So how do we do this? Well, we can create an Emotions Class for ourselves right now. No time like the present. We can set aside some time and space each day and begin a daily practice of WELCOME-ing in feeling. We can become mindful and intentional humans, committed to embracing and choosing feeling over not feeling.

Let's WELCOME in feeling. We can use this WELCOME acronym as a guideline for cultivating a new inner environment – one that opens us up to increased feeling and encourages us to stay with and outlast our emotions. Let's exercise our feeling muscle.

- *W – **Welcome*** feelings when they arise within you.
- *E – **Embody*** the feeling, allow the feeling to be a sensate and real inner experience – this is **felt emotion.**
- *L – **Let go*** of any resistance and tension to the feeling in both your body and mind.
- *C – **Check in*** with yourself to see if you have time to stay with the feeling.
- *O – **Open yourself*** to staying with and riding the feeling from beginning to end or until it shifts by changing shape, location, or intensity.
- *M – **Move toward*** your body and away from your thoughts and try not to analyze or assign meaning to the feeling.
- *E – **Embrace*** your Neutral Observer and observe yourself through a nonjudgmental and accepting lens.

This WELCOME checklist is a tool. It can become your new "feelings" toolbox that reminds you to nurture an inner climate that can stay with and tolerate feelings – all feelings, whether they are hard or lovely or painful or pleasurable. This checklist is important because you can use it and reuse it again and again.

Sometimes, we will not have the time, energy, or bandwidth to stay with feelings, but we can always try again next time. Remember, the fact that there will always be another feeling right around the corner is one of the most predictable things about emotions. There is always another opportunity to practice staying with feelings.

We will play with this WELCOME acronym later in this chapter, but first a moment of caution.

WHEN FEELINGS AREN'T WELCOME

In the preface, I explained that this book is not specifically intended for individuals who have experienced significant trauma, as there are many research-based therapeutics that are readily available for trauma survivors. And yet, as I said before, I do not discourage anyone from reading this book; rather, I recommend that individuals with a history of trauma have trauma-informed healthcare providers, therapists, or doctors to support them while doing so.

While writing this book, I attended a workshop at Kripalu, a yoga and meditation retreat in the Berkshires of Massachusetts. I befriended a licensed social worker who had recently attended a yoga and trauma workshop. When I told her about the book I was writing, she was both intrigued and concerned. "What about triggering or re-experiencing feelings of trauma?" she asked.

I explained to her that I was keenly aware of re-experiencing trauma, and in fact, it had derailed me from writing this book for many years. I further explained that I work with trauma patients, using bodywork to elicit deeper feeling, but I have always had the ability to review and ensure that each individual I was working with had significant therapy under their belt, understood that the work could bring up very difficult feelings, and had a current therapist and/or support network in place. As a clinician, there is a difference between having confidence that a patient is supported both by your own work and that of other licensed mental health providers and putting ideas out into the world in a book for folks to explore on their own.

When I work with patients with complex traumatic histories, the development of a safe therapeutic relationship is incredibly important. Traumatic feelings, memories, and experiences can resurface. My patients need to feel that the four walls of my office (as well as the four legs of my table) are a safe place to land, meaning that trust and safety must be established before "feeling" work can begin. Additionally, that trust must be authentic.

Some questions to ask ourselves when we enter the pursuit of deeper feeling:

- Are we better equipped (physically, mentally, emotionally, spiritually) in our current lives to handle very difficult feelings if they resurface from an earlier part of our lives?
- Are we in a better, more centered, and more stable place in our lives to handle revisiting challenging feelings?
- Do we have a strong support network (family, friends, therapists, doctors, therapeutic groups) in our current lives?
- Do we have grounding, calming, or centering practices that allow us to land and feel connected to the earth, our lives, and those we care about?

These are questions to ask ourselves when we want to stay with and outlast difficult feelings. Remember, the body does the feeling, and similarly, it holds the feelings. It is imperative that we understand that, just as we push a feeling of rejection under the surface, we bury memories of painful and traumatic experiences.

Those of us who work with trauma must unequivocally honor the feelings and memories that an individual has buried. We must respect and revere everyone's past experiences, as well as understand that individuals coped with past trauma in the best way that they could have at the time. With that respect comes an understanding that for every holding, every numbing, and every buried feeling that we carry with us, there is a reason for it, an experience behind it, and a purpose that the holding or numbing has served in our lives. We acknowledge, with profound reverence, that burying those experiences was both a way to survive and a way to move forward in life at the time.

When we wish to open to hard feelings and holdings in the body, it is important to acknowledge that we are in a different time, a different place, and many times, we are very different people than when the original experience or trauma found us. With more insight, therapy, and experience, we may be better equipped to deal with that original experience. If we are not in a better place, better equipped, or better supported, I recommend holding off exploring, or WELCOME-ing, deeper feeling until a different time.

For individuals who are ready to begin the process of tolerating painful feelings, there is an inner trust that is built by practice and learned experience – a learning that they can survive difficult feelings.

My choice of the word "surviving" may initially appear hyperbolic, and yet, if we remember Ellen from the last chapter, my clinical experience has proven otherwise. The fear that we will not survive our feelings, while sounding silly or absurd at face value, is far from uncommon. I have had numerous patients over the years who got to the edge of a hard feeling and would pull back because it felt too threatening or terrifying. Feelings can be scary, and when we don't know or trust that we can make it through to the other side of them, we sense danger and resist the feeling. For individuals who have endured trauma, their feelings can very rightly evoke signals of threat and danger.

This is why starting with less threatening but still uncomfortable feelings – like loneliness, rejection, and jealousy – is recommended first. Remember the concept and framework of practicing emotions in our hypothetical childhood Emotions Class. Practicing is important. Practicing exercises and tones our feeling muscle. As we practice sitting with smaller, less daunting, and less threatening feelings, we increase our capacity to stay with harder, more painful ones.

In other words, before re-awaking older, more elusive, and hidden feelings, we can begin by opening up to our day-to-day frustrations, regrets, insecurities, disappointments, embarrassments, and feelings of failure. While not easy or pleasurable, these uncomfortable feelings are a place to start and the place to practice. Learning to tolerate uncomfortable feelings and ride their waves – however long or short, intense or bumpy – is where the work starts.

Patients with a history of trauma can, for sure, participate in this process, as we all can use practice in staying with hard feelings in our day-to-day lives. However, we need to be careful to understand that WELCOME-ing felt emotion may trigger and resurface old feelings. I can't overstate enough that a safe and supportive network is imperative. In my experience, when someone knows that they are supported and is not surprised by a resurfacing of old pain, they can work through it and feel it. It is the unsupported surprises that can disarm us and upend our lives.

A MISUNDERSTANDING OF TOLERATING DISCOMFORT

For some individuals, the concept of staying with and tolerating discomfort leads to misunderstanding. It is important for all of us to understand the distinction between staying with painful feelings/ emotions and staying in a situation/relationship that causes pain. This may, at first glance, seem like two very different ideas, but when we are living in emotionally or physically toxic situations, those lines are blurred.

Staying with and getting to the other side of a feeling is constructive and instructive. We learn a new behavior or skill, and we see that we can feel hard feelings, and then they pass; we grow more resilient because we are not daunted or controlled by our emotions and thus approach felt emotion with familiarity, confidence, and trust.

Staying in or tolerating a relationship, a living situation, or an experience that causes emotional or physical pain must be approached in a completely different manner. Please be clear that *The Feeling Muscle* is not promoting the idea of tolerating or staying with the discomfort or pain of being in a toxic or abusive situation or relationship.

BODY BREAK

Take a moment and bring your attention to your breath. Place one of your hands on your belly. Gently and softly breathe into your belly and your hand. Resist questioning or judging yourself; there is no right or wrong way to do the exercise. Allow your inhale and exhale to be easy. Breathe into your hand that rests on your belly. Let your belly gently expand with each inhale and relax with each exhale. Stay with your breath for a few minutes. That's all.

LARS: RAISED TO FREEZE HIS FEELINGS

Lars was an elementary school teacher and coach who came to my office because he was anxious and worried. Both his therapist and internist had diagnosed him with panic attacks.

The attacks often occurred while he was driving, and Lars had a long commute to work, as the school system he worked for was a distance from his home. Because of his commute, his panic attacks were not just an unfortunate situation, but a daily obstacle. A few days prior to our first appointment, he had decided not to go to work because he feared having a panic attack. And the next day, he got off the highway and drove home on backroads, taking him over an hour out of his way, just to avoid a particular patch of highway that he believed triggered his attacks.

Lars had been in therapy, and as a result, he was very open with me about his past history, which was complex. Lars's father was an alcoholic. Lars had explored with his therapist his constant fear as a child that his father might harm his mother, his siblings, or himself. In a recent therapy session, he had uncovered a significant piece of insight. His father had screamed at him and punished him using physical force whenever Lars showed anger or frustration as a child, and Lars made the connection between these traumatic childhood experiences and how he had shut down his feelings, especially those of anger, as an adult. He was excited about making these connections and was convinced that this shutdown was connected to his panic attacks.

Lars had heard about my bodywork and had had the remarkable insight that there was something in his body that he might be holding. He believed it was a piece of the puzzle for him – an important clue to freeing himself from panic. Our first few sessions were spent getting to know each other, and Lars getting to know my bodywork.

We started with a body scan. Sometimes, when the body scan gets to the abdomen and chest, I will ask my patients to "tighten and then release their breath." This request elicits both fun and funny responses at times and, in the process, reveals some interesting things about my patients' breath. Lars noticed almost immediately that his breath was "pretty tight," even before he tried to tighten it.

I had indeed noticed that the area of Lars's body where his diaphragm sat was rock solid and held tight. And his breaths were so small that I could tell he needed to take more breaths per minute to make up for his very shallow and tight inhales. His exhales were almost imperceptible, save for a very large and labored exhale roughly every four or five minutes, which seemed to be making up for all the lost opportunities to let the air out. Lars's breathing was very restricted, so much so that barely any motion was perceptible through his ribcage and diaphragm.

While I had simply noticed this phenomenon in our first session, our second session allowed for a little more attention and exploration of his diaphragmatic region. After a shorter body scan, I placed my hands directly on the area where the lower ribcage and abdomen meet. I encouraged him to "feel himself" under my hands, and after a few moments, I asked him what, if anything, he was feeling.

He told me that he didn't feel anything in that area. It feels like a "no man's land" – those were the words he used. I asked him to stay with that awareness, and I repeated his words, "no man's land." A few minutes later, he said, "I'm frustrated because I don't feel anything there!"

In these moments when patients are frustrated that they can't feel themselves, I will simply tell them what I am feeling under my hands. I told Lars that I felt his diaphragm region to be like a tight elastic band, both taut yet stretched to its limit. Just those few words elicited a somewhat deeper and more relaxed breath. "Yes, I feel that too," he said. It was almost as if I gave him permission to feel something within himself.

At the end of that session, I gave Lars some homework. He was to imagine his breath as an ocean wave. I explained that just like we don't have control over the waves of the ocean, I wanted him to approach his breath with a similar detachment. Meaning that he would observe each breath as it comes upon him, resisting an urge to change or control his breathing. (The full exercise is detailed in Chapter Seven's experiential section.)

Lars returned for a few more bodywork sessions, and he was very diligent with his breath visualization homework. During one table session, Lars gleaned a remarkable insight. He remembered that he used to hide in his room when his father came home drunk. He remembered that he would hold his breath, anticipating some sort of conflict, until his father would either lie down and fall asleep or sit down to watch TV. Lars would stay stiff and frozen in his room; he would not just hold his breath, but he would freeze his emotions and his body as well.

Lars had the remarkable insight that he was, in essence, still holding his breath — still, to this day, freezing his body and his emotions too. He told me that he had been taught to freeze his emotions from an early age, as it had felt like life or death in those tense, scary moments when his father would return home. Remember, when our body senses danger, we often freeze.

At our next session, Lars came into my office with a burst of energy. He said he had had a thought that he wanted to talk about. "I haven't had a panic attack in about a month. You know, I have been holding back my breath and my emotions for so long, I wonder if my panic attacks have been a way for them to come out, or something like that?"

I told Lars that I couldn't answer his question for sure, but that it sounded like a remarkable insight. "Our bodies are extraordinary," I replied. "It sounds like your body and your intuition are speaking to you."

Lars remarked that the breath/wave exercise had shown him how much he had held and controlled his breath throughout his life. "It's amazing how focusing on my breathing has transformed my life," Lars excitedly reported.

Lars committed to continuing his breath exercises and his work with his therapist. I saw him again for a handful of bodywork sessions over the course of a few months. Admittedly, I have lost touch with Lars, but from the time that he took that larger exhale on my table, coupled with his memories and insight in that moment, he never reported another panic attack to me. There was plenty of work left for Lars to do. We are all works in progress. But his new breathing practice and his remarkable insights helped to create a significant shift for Lars – a shift that was transformational.

TRYING TO OUTRUN OUR FEELINGS: YOU CAN RUN, BUT YOU CANNOT HIDE

We all know that if you ignore someone long enough, they usually get the hint and go away. We treat our feelings much like this too, but there is one difference. If we ignore or avoid our feelings long enough, they don't just go away, they get buried within us. Sometimes right below the surface. Sometimes they bury themselves very deep down. There is an inconvenient truth about feeling our emotions, or rather not feeling them. We may think we can outrun feelings, we may think we can stuff them or swallow them, we may think we can numb them, but they don't just miraculously disappear. They stay within us – deep within us.

Feelings do catch up to us. A child's (or adult's, for that matter) anxiety can come out as trouble falling asleep. We see feelings catching up with us in situations of extreme rage, where pent-up anger can come out in violent and dangerous behavior. We see traumatic experiences get stored within our psyche and body and come out as physical pain, emotional shutdown, or acting out.

Sometimes, we try to outrun feelings by only talking about them. Talking about feelings can be a huge relief and a significant release, but for many of us, talking about feelings is just part of the process. Pretending that we live from the neck up and that our bodies just get us from place A to place B won't cut it here. We can't hide from our bodies, and we can't hide from our feelings.

When I was a dancer living in New York City, I lived with a certain amount of daily pain. A few bad falls as a young gymnast and years of overtraining and improper training as a dancer had left me crooked and misaligned. This misalignment combined with my tendency to tense my body and hold my breath – my body armor – created a significant amount of discomfort that I carried with me day to day.

Thanks to the wise advice of a dance teacher, in my early twenties, I began weekly sessions with an Alexander Technique teacher. If you are unfamiliar with the Alexander Technique, it is a form of bodywork – a movement reeducation technique that involves private lessons in posture and body usage; in short, students can learn to use their bodies more efficiently, improve posture, and reduce habitual tension.

I remember one particular session when my teacher noticed and remarked that I held quite a lot of tension in my sternum. It struck me as an odd comment to make, as I had never really considered that part of body – my sternum – as being of much importance. In fact, as she made the comment, I remember thinking to myself, my sternum, really? I can't even feel my sternum. I shifted my eyes downward to see where she was touching, just to make sure I really existed there.

That numbness and disassociation should have been a sign to me that something was afoot.

When we got to the portion of the lesson where I was to lie on the bodywork table, she placed one hand on my sternum and one hand directly opposite my sternum, on my back, right between my shoulder blades. Her hands paused in this position for several minutes. She just stayed with me; her hands were mirrors of each other with my sternum in between.

Out of the blue and catching me off guard, I felt as if my breath was taken away from me. In an instant, I froze between her hands. I was paralyzed for what seemed like minutes, but what was probably only seconds. A powerful, overwhelming feeling came over me. I searched inside myself for what was going on. What was I feeling? This feeling was not familiar to me at all. It took my breath away.

As this was early in my experience with bodywork, I kept it to myself. Instead of telling my teacher what I was feeling, I held my breath even tighter to see if I could stave off this new feeling. The power of sharing my experience on the table – or the idea that my feelings could be validated by being seen and heard – was foreign to me at the time. So, I said nothing. I did nothing. The session wrapped up, and I quickly got off the table. I left the room with a quick and curt farewell, all the while holding my breath and body tight.

I took the elevator down to the street below. As I exited the building doors, I gasped as if taking a breath after a deep dive. I fled to the side of the building as I burst into tears and rushed for a side street, one that was less crowded so I could avoid being noticed. I couldn't stop. I couldn't control myself. Hot tears were streaming down my face. My breathing was loud and irregular.

Nothing about this was familiar. Nothing about this was normal for me. Nothing about this made sense. I was normally held tight. My emotions were usually well guarded and kept in check. Something had surfaced. Something deep and powerful and real had awoken from within me.

I walked home that night, although I don't remember exactly how I made it to my West Village stoop. From my tense, rigid, and numb sternum had come an unexpected tsunami of sadness that carried me all the way home. My tears never ceased until I reached my fifth-floor walk-up, my tiny studio apartment whose four walls protected me from the outside world. I turned the key, opened the door, and fell to my knees. An overwhelming and unending feeling of sadness overtook me. Sadness for what, I couldn't be sure in that moment. But it was an old and deep sadness – a sadness that I could not run from. Not anymore.

IT TAKES PRACTICE!

Beginning a daily commitment to deeper feeling involves practice. A cool thing about practicing felt emotion is that there are lots of opportunities to do so. If we miss one, we can catch another feeling in short order.

In mind-body medicine, we use the term "practice" as both a verb and a noun. We "practice" our techniques and tools, and we create and commit to a daily "practice." For some, a daily practice may be a gratitude practice, where we list three things we are grateful for about the day or keep a journal to jot down things we are appreciative of in our lives. If we commit to a daily practice, we commit to doing something day after day with the intention that it becomes an integral, consistent, and lasting part of our lives.

By practicing the WELCOME acronym from earlier in this chapter, you start a daily practice of opening yourself to deeper feeling. You create an inner environment that WELCOMEs feelings within you and nurtures your feeling muscle. Maybe you commit to it once or twice a day, welcoming in one feeling and staying with it. The "W" – **Welcome feelings when they arise within you** – is where you start: Welcoming in a single feeling and staying with it.

The "E" is your felt emotion. **Embody the feeling, allow the feeling to be a sensate and real inner experience.** Let your emotions take shape in your body. Remind yourself that felt emotion is tangible and discernible. It has form, intensity, and density. Trust that feeling is the body's job.

The "L" is tricky for many. **Let go of any resistance and tension to the feeling in both your body and mind.** Letting go of the resistance to deeper feeling is challenging, especially when you may have built emotional dams or engaged in numbing behaviors. Remember, your body armor is part of your resistance. For anyone who has tried to release body armor, you know that it is a tall order, but so worthwhile. Note that your Inner Critic is part of your resistance too; thoughts filled with judgment and criticism build mental armor between you and feeling your feelings freely. Letting go of resistance takes awareness and commitment. It takes practice.

It is hard to find the time or the space in your busy life for the "C." **Check in with yourself to see if you have time to stay with the feeling.** This might be the toughest part for you. Can you find a way to check in with yourself on a daily basis? Can you get in the habit of asking yourself, "Do I have time to stay with this feeling? Can I take a minute and pause what I am doing to ride this feeling?"

The lifespan of some feelings will be brief, easy to ride out, and satisfying because they fade away. The lifespan of other feelings may be more drawn out. Maybe the feeling shapeshifts to another feeling. Maybe the feeling lingers in the swell or crescendo, which can make riding the wave more challenging. However, the more you practice sitting with emotions, the more familiar and comfortable you will become playing in your waves.

How willing and open are you to riding the wave? The "O" is not easy, for staying with a feeling can be unbearable. **Open yourself to staying with and riding the feeling from beginning to end or until it shifts by changing shape, location, or intensity.** Remember that emotions can shapeshift; sometimes, riding a wave means that you ride it until it completely fades away, and sometimes, you ride it until it changes to a distinctly different feeling.

Do you recall when you were asked to take note of two very different feelings? You visualized what it feels like in your body to move forward with a parking brake on. And then you imagined what riding a wave without effort or resistance felt like inside. These two very different experiences in your body illustrate the effort and energy it takes to hold back or bottle up emotions compared to opening up. Opening yourself to feeling means riding the wave, surrendering to the dynamic flow of emotion.

The "M" is so hard sometimes. **Move toward your body and away from your thoughts and try not to analyze or assign meaning to the feeling.** This concept may go against your upbringing, your habits, and your behaviors. It is engrained in our culture to stay with our thoughts and to live in our heads and our minds. Try to avoid analyzing and attaching meaning to the feeling; there is plenty of time to bring thought into the mix. Try to make your WELCOME time solely about the body's experience.

The "E" is where you foster and nurture your Neutral Observer. **Embrace your Neutral Observer and observe yourself through a nonjudgmental and accepting lens.** While the Inner Critic takes you into your thoughts, observing your felt emotion keeps you in your body. Observing yourself with loving kindness does not come naturally. It takes self-awareness and persistence to thwart the Inner Critic. It takes practice.

We must be tenacious in our dedication to felt emotion, as we devote some time and some space to the process every day. In public or private. On a walk or in the shower. In the arms of a loved one or alone in a room. Welcoming in feeling may or may not feel good. It may feel like a much-needed release, an inconvenience, or a ridiculous waste of time. But here's the rub. It's a part of living, a part of being human. And whether we like it or not, we are the only ones who can feel our feelings. No one else can feel them for us, and no one else can take them away. Feeling our feelings is our job to do.

WANT AN EXCUSE TO GO TO THE MOVIES? OR A ROCK CONCERT? OR AN ART GALLERY?

One of my favorite ways to practice felt emotion is both fun and entertaining. We have talked a lot about staying with hard, challenging, and painful feelings. But it doesn't always have to be hard work.

For many of us, art stirs and evokes deep feeling and emotion within us. Whether it is opera, music, film, visual art, or poetry, art touches us profoundly.

Think about a time when...

- A movie brought you to tears or a painting stirred a longing within you

- A song brought up an intimate memory or dancing filled you with joy
- A book filled you with heartache or music stopped you in your tracks
- A photo took your breath away or a poem made you blush

Art moves something in us that resonates with deep feeling. We align in some way with the frequency of a melody, a message, a movement. We are impacted by an image or a scene. Art speaks to and touches our souls.

For many years, I worked with Kenneth, an engineer. I mention that Kenneth was an engineer because he was very intellectual and very conceptual. He was careful and thoughtful with everything he told me, as if he meticulously considered what he would say before actually saying it. In the years we worked together, Kenneth would often tell me that he was perplexed by the fact that he would always cry during a particular scene in *Marley and Me*. After about the fourth or fifth time Kenneth mentioned that he had watched the movie, I asked him if he had any idea why he put the movie on so much. After thinking about it, he pondered, "Maybe because I need a good cry?" Kenneth's wide smile and deep belly laugh clued me into the fact that he might be on to something.

Theater and movies can reenact scenes that feel familiar to us, and they can evoke feelings that are familiar. Books and films can create unfamiliar scenarios that summon emotions that we don't feel that often; perhaps these are feelings that we need to practice. I'm quite certain that one of the reasons that teenagers listen to music in their rooms is that it helps them feel something strongly. Books can bring up feelings that resonate with our best selves and our worst selves. Photographs can mirror our feelings. Paintings can initiate and instigate deep feeling. Poetry may stir angst or hope within us.

Since I can remember, I have had an unapologetic love of show tunes. My father, an artist, actor, and director, introduced me to *My Fair Lady, Oklahoma!, The Music Man* and many more Broadway musicals, as he played records while painting in his studio. I would play happily and calmly right below his easel, and we would take in the music together.

We watched many Broadway musicals together, sitting mesmerized side by side. One of the last memories I have of my dad is opening the door to his car and being greeted by *The Phantom of the Opera* blasting from his minivan's stereo system. The very last time I saw my dad was at Goodspeed Opera House. I said my last goodbye, unbeknownst to me at the time, after seeing *Seven Brides for Seven Brothers* together side by side.

To this day, show tunes evoke such strong feelings inside me. Feelings of happiness, loss, safety, connection, grief, and warmth. Luckily, I subscribe to a Broadway radio station in my car. Whenever I want to remember my dad or feel strong feelings of love and loss, all I have to do is turn up the volume.

So, if you don't already have an excuse to visit an art museum, start a new book, or buy a ticket to the theater or symphony, consider this your excuse. Dig up that old mix tape that filled you with youthful desire or teenage angst. Revisit a movie that you know brought on big feelings. Maybe find a stashed love note or poem from an old lover. Buy a ticket to a rock concert. Check it off your bucket list and go to the opera for the first time. And practice feeling freely and deeply.

CHAPTER EIGHT EXPERIENTIAL

I. BODY PLAY: WELCOME-ing IN FEELING

Make a commitment to WELCOME in a new feeling each day. There are many ways to approach this commitment. One approach is to go about your day as usual, and when and if a noticeable feeling comes upon you, you can pause what you are doing (if you have the time and are able) and use your WELCOME checklist. Another approach is to set aside time each day to check in and see if anything is brewing. You may want to use this guided imagery script to start your practice each day; you can record your voice reading this script and play it back while you are resting or meditating.

> *Begin by finding a comfortable position: sitting, lying on the floor or a mat, or resting in a supported manner. Your eyes may be open or closed. Take a few moments to feel your body. Scan your body from head to toe to notice areas of tension, gripping, or holding as well as areas of releasing or softening.*
>
> *As your awareness shifts more toward your inner experiences, observe if there is an inner feeling that wants your attention. You can even say out loud or to yourself, "I am present. Is there an inner feeling that is speaking to me? I am present and listening."*

When you have identified a feeling that is present within you, welcome the feeling into your body. Try to avoid having any agenda and resist approaching the feeling with judgment or criticism. Try not to label, analyze, or explain the feeling.

Greet the feeling as if you are shaking its hand or opening the front door to it. Invite the feeling to stay awhile. Give the feeling your full attention by staying with it.

Use your checklist…

- **W – Welcome** feelings when they arise within you.
- **E – Embody** the feeling. Allow the feeling to be a tangible and real inner experience.
- **L – Let go** of any resistance and tension to the feeling in both your body and mind.
- **C – Check in** with yourself to see if you have time to stay with the feeling.
- **O – Open yourself** to staying with and riding the feeling from beginning to end or until it changes shape, location, or intensity.
- **M – Move toward** your body and away from your thoughts and try not to analyze or assign meaning to the feeling.
- **E – Embrace** your Neutral Observer and observe yourself through a nonjudgmental and accepting lens.

EXPERIENTIAL

2. PRACTICE EMOTION

Choose a visual art form or a particular film, book, song, passage, etc. that you know moves you with strong emotion. Engage with whatever form of art you choose and WELCOME in the feelings that are stirred or moved within you. That's all.

3. "WELCOME-ing IN FEELING" PROMPT

Use this statement as a springboard for a journal entry, a short story, a painting/picture, a meditation, a poem, a song, a dance, or any form of creative expression. Express as much detail as possible.

I welcomed in a hard feeling. I outlasted a hard feeling. My inner experience was...

CHAPTER NINE

TAKING RESPONSIBILITY FOR OUR FEELINGS

After fifteen years of private practice, I took a sabbatical and moved abroad with my family. A few months before we moved, my mom – an extraordinary woman and grounding force in my life – was diagnosed with pancreatic cancer. Initially, it looked like she would beat the cancer, but that was not to be. Weeks after she died, my family lived through a hellishly restrictive COVID-19 lockdown in Spain; we could not leave our apartment for months, and we were isolated and frightened in a way we had never imagined.

I attempted to manage my feelings with emotional grace and aplomb. I did not. My emotions were wild; so many big and terrifying feelings overflowed my meager and exhausted inner container. I had no strength or resilience to hold space for the loss of my mom and the terror of living through a COVID lockdown abroad. More often than I care to admit, I spewed out and unloaded my emotions all over my family. I was not taking responsibility for my feelings; rather, I was discharging them and displacing them on the people I loved the most.

NO ONE CAN DO THE FEELING FOR US

We are the only ones who can feel our feelings. Sometimes, we are fortunate enough to have another person or persons who can help hold the space for our feelings; they may do this by being present with us, by listening to us, or by showing kindness, love, and support. But often, we do not.

Let me be clear: we are not always responsible for the pain that we hold, but we are responsible for the pain that is released, because we are the ones who must bear it and feel it. The universal truth – that no one can feel our feelings for us – can feel soul-crushing because some of us know that we hold feelings or have feelings that we'd rather not acknowledge, let alone feel. When we understand that we are the only ones who can ride out our difficult emotions, we face a turning point – can we withstand and outlast our painful feelings?

Taking responsibility for our feelings frees those emotions and breathes life into them. Rather than tensing and guarding against unwanted emotions surfacing, we take up space in our world, and we regain some power over our challenging and difficult times.

It is true. We cannot enlist someone else to feel for us. Because we are human, we accept that living entails a certain amount of suffering and pain, of which emotional pain and felt emotion are indeed a part. Maybe my WELCOME acronym feels unrealistic when affixed to our more painful and tormented suffering; however, we can be present to our suffering in fits and spurts. We can.

When my mother was dying, I made a pact with myself. My father had died suddenly and unexpectedly fifteen years earlier, and during the months following my dad's death, I was numb. I am not criticizing or judging my emotional numbness. That's just how it was. I was not present with my grief after my father died, and I would experience panic attacks at random and unexpected times; I believe these attacks were a result of my inability to process and feel all the complicated feelings of this foundational loss – fear, guilt, confusion, anger, despair, and profound sadness. Again, I'm not judging my behavior, rather I am simply recognizing and validating how I emotionally navigated my dad's death.

But when it came time for my mother to live her last months, I committed to something different. I had been through the death of a parent, so I had a bit of a roadmap. I told myself that I would be as present as possible during that time. Present to my feelings – my felt love for her, my felt grief, my felt fear, and my felt heartache. I would be present in my conversations with my mother. I would tell her everything I wanted and needed her to hear. And in turn and of equal importance, I would be present for her – for what she needed to say or feel.

Some moments, I stayed true to that commitment, and other times, I did not. And that's okay. I knew I was the only one who could feel what brewed inside me, and I stayed with it at times. I had to let it flow through me at times. Because it was real and undulating and powerful. Because at the time I was essentially commuting between

Barcelona, Spain and Houston, Texas, I felt a lot of feelings in airports and on airplanes. Quite often, my grief would overflow as I transitioned from caring for my mother to returning to my family, as if the time and space in between those two aspects of my life was a place I could truly let myself feel. Whether it was quiet tears, deep pain in my heart, or audible sobs, my feelings of love and loss would take shape and release as I waited in airport terminals and as I traveled across the Atlantic Ocean.

I can't say it felt good to feel my grief, but I can say that I felt connected with what was transpiring in my life; that connection grounded me to a deep acceptance and honoring of my suffering. I was losing a parent, my last parent, and life would never, ever be the same.

I am not alone in the conundrum of how to navigate the death of a most cherished person. We have all lived through loss and suffering of some sort. However, we can be living proof that if we stay open and grounded in some of those moments, we can come out the other end with a deeper understanding of human suffering. And that deeper understanding often leads to more empathy, wisdom, and insight in our lives – three things we can use more of in the world.

DISPLACING AND DUMPING OUR FEELINGS ON OTHERS

Maybe someday we will be able to measure or quantify what burying feelings does to our health and wellbeing. For now, we can only suppose. I do know that when we tuck feelings away, we run the risk of letting those feelings out, as they bubble up, on the ones we love.

In the last few chapters, we have explored the idea that when we don't fully feel or process what lies within us, it does not move through us. It stays with us as we go about our jobs, our education, and our lives. Feelings are an energy that is meant to flow and release. Remember the parking brake vs. riding the wave. Stuck and held energy just builds up. Our tense muscles and held breath might contain the energy, for the time being, but it is still there. Until we can't hold it back anymore.

It is tempting and sometimes convenient to put our feelings on others, to blame others, and to throw our feelings out into the world. But it's not fair. The raw truth is that it may feel good to get it out, but if you don't want to feel it, why would anyone else? Why should someone else be subjected to the feelings you don't want to feel?

Have you ever...

- Felt so anxious that you dumped that anxiety on your family or felt so angry that you raged at your partner?
- Felt so overwhelmed that you upset a friend by your behavior or felt so powerless that you lashed out at another person?
- Felt so inadequate that you used harsh words to make someone else feel bad about themselves or felt so much shame that you shamed someone else?
- Felt so alone that your behavior pushed someone away or felt so frustrated that you barked at your kids?

This displacement of feelings is really common, so common, in fact, that most of the time, we do it in a mindless, unconscious manner. When we feel something bubble up, we push it down within us or eject it out into the world around us – which usually means those we love and care about.

The fact that we would rather put our feelings out into the world than feel them ourselves is more proof of how hard it is to tolerate feelings within ourselves. It's a quick fix to displace feelings on others, but as I have said before, it is unfair. Let's do the hard work of owning our feelings instead.

EXPANDING OUR INNER CONTAINERS

The term or image of a container can be useful to explain how we hold feelings within ourselves. In both mind-body and psychological circles, some like to imagine or visualize that we are containers that hold space for our many feelings. Like the feeling muscle, the container is a metaphor; both our inner container and our feeling muscle are ways to represent our body's emotional intelligence and resilience. When we are anxious, stressed, and overwhelmed, our container may shrink, and our feelings can overflow; our ability to hold, process, and feel powerful feelings diminishes, and our feelings spill over into the world around us.

Our containers can be small for reasons that we have already talked about: a wariness about feeling and expressing emotions, messages from society and caregivers that place judgment on feeling, and not making feeling a priority. Our reliance on mindless distractions also compromises our containers because if we are constantly distracted, we don't get much of a chance to practice holding feelings. All of these forces contribute to our inner containers being too small and meager to hold our many feelings.

So, how do we expand our container? How do we renovate our containers so they are roomy, flexible, and inviting, so they can take in and fit all our feelings? Well, we have learned just that by reading this book and engaging in the experiential exercises at the end of each chapter.

Let's take a moment to recap the key points of this book, as we look through the lens of expanding and renovating our inner containers to hold, withstand, and ride out feelings:

- We accept and acknowledge that feelings are felt by the body and in the body – our felt emotion. Felt emotion is a real and valid part of being human.
- We understand that we run from, avoid, or numb our painful and hard emotions in a variety of ways. We may hide or bury some of our painful feelings deep within us.
- We may be wary of feelings because of societal messages, upbringings, and an emphasis on thinking.
- We can experience how felt emotion is like a wave, with an ebb and flow, possibly a change in shape, and a beginning and an end.
- We can notice that tension, guarding, and holding our breath are

ways we create body armor and push away, swallow, and stuff down felt emotion.

- We can embrace new concepts like living more in our bodies and less in our thoughts as well as adopting and fostering a neutral and nonjudgmental attitude.
- We understand that we are the only ones who can feel our feelings; we cannot enlist others to feel for us.

In essence, this book provides a map and guide to expanding our container. When we expand and grow our containers, we can hold our feelings with an acceptance and a nonjudgmental approach that allows us the time and space to feel them. Our newly revamped and renovated container has space for feelings to spread out and move about; it has plenty of room for waves to unfold and storms to bluster.

Our container has no agenda and rejects critical thoughts. Our container is pliable and flexible. It can change shape as our feelings change shape. Our inner container is a gauge of our inner resilience; the more room we make for weathering any emotion, the more unflappable we become in the face of stormy, unpredictable times.

LYDIA: IT FEELS TOO MESSY

Lydia was a physical therapist who loved her work. She came to see me initially for insomnia, but in time, she shared that she struggled with significant anxiety and perfectionism. Lydia was both thoughtful and insightful, and found our discussions of the mind-body connection fascinating.

Lydia had had a very unpredictable childhood. Her father was an alcoholic, and her parents had had a messy divorce when she was a baby. Her life had been chaotic as she got shuffled from one parent's home to the next. Lydia was an only child, and she described many a situation in her childhood when she was left to fend for herself or where she was expected to take care of her father. As a result, she was mature beyond her years, and yet she struggled to tolerate any unpredictability within her life.

Lydia found bodywork very relaxing, and she was very content learning relaxation and breathing techniques to employ when she was feeling stressed and overwhelmed, which was quite often. The herbal remedy I recommended for her insomnia combined with relaxation exercises before bed had significantly improved the quality of her sleep. After this improvement in her health, I didn't see Lydia for nearly three years.

Then Lydia called unexpectedly one day and wanted to make an appointment. Her life had gotten complicated. She had moved in with her boyfriend, and her current job was very demanding. Her new living situation was triggering feelings of unpredictability that harkened back to her childhood. Lydia was feeling pulled in many directions; she was under enormous pressure at work and was experiencing feelings that she articulated as "not in control of my life."

Before getting on the table, we discussed the possibility of working at a "feelings" level rather than simply a relaxation level. She was open to it. After a few moments of a body scan to bring her both into the moment and into her body, I asked her if there were any noticeable sensations in her body, as if her body might be speaking to her.

"My chest is really tight," she said. "And my shoulders feel like boulders attached to me." I asked her if she could stay with the tightness. And I put my hands gently on her shoulders – her boulders.

I noticed that placing my hands on her shoulders pulled Lydia back into her thoughts, as she immediately started speaking to me in a restless manner. This shift in Lydia alerted me to the fact that she didn't want to feel the boulders. As Lydia talked rapidly, her breathing became quicker and more shallow.

"Our apartment is a mess. I can't keep things organized living with another person. Things aren't where I put them. The forks were in the wrong drawer this morning." I listened quietly with my hands still on her shoulders. "Work is crazy too," she whispered in a hush that illustrated how exhausting it all was for her.

I validated her words. "Work is crazy, and the forks were in the wrong drawer this morning," I repeated. Lydia took a softer and wider breath as if in agreement.

I slowly shifted my right hand to her sternum. My left hand remained on her left shoulder. I asked her if she could feel herself under my hands. "Take your time," I said. "Remember, there is no right or wrong on the table. There is no judgment and no agenda. Just notice yourself under my hands."

> "It feels so heavy and busy under my sternum. It feels too messy," Lydia said after a minute or two. "It feels too messy. I don't like it."

> "It's messy. You don't like the feeling," I repeated.

> "Yes, the feeling. I don't want to feel it. I don't like it," Lydia said in a sharper and harsher tone than usual.

> "Are you able to stay with it for a bit? The messy feeling?" I asked.

Lydia paused, but quietly nodded, signaling that she could. We stayed there together for many minutes, with her messy feeling, as it moved through her.

> "The feeling has softened a bit," Lydia said. "It doesn't feel as bad anymore."

That day's bodywork concluded with Lydia taking a breath and moving off the table rather carefully and slowly, almost as if she was moving in a kinder, gentler way.

I checked in with Lydia before she left. Sitting in a chair, at a distance from the table, Lydia said, "That messiness is what I felt as a kid. I had no control of things. I guess I'm feeling that way in my life right now."

We talked briefly about how old feelings can be triggered. Even though she didn't like to feel the messiness, she knew that messiness was a part of life. She also had the insight that she would need to be okay with a certain amount of messiness if she wanted to share her life with another person.

"I can't be in control of where the forks are all the time," Lydia said. She left my office with a smile on her face, almost a chuckle at her lack of control over the forks. Even though she didn't like the feeling, not at all, a part of her knew her insight would spark growth in herself and her relationship.

This session opened a door for Lydia and for future conversations and table sessions where we would explore the idea of her holding space for messiness. And for her to recognize, practice, and trust that she could move through and outlast an uncomfortable feeling, one she "did not like."

In essence, Lydia knew that her container would have to adapt to hold hard, messy feelings. This awareness was just the beginning for Lydia. She would go on to be tested many, many times with more messy stuff and more messy situations and more messy feelings. Such is life. And sometimes, she would stay with the feeling of messiness inside, and sometimes, she would run away from the feeling as fast as she could. Yet one thing was for sure: she would have many more opportunities to practice.

BODY BREAK

If you are able, put the book down and take a short walk. Perhaps the walk is up and down a flight of stairs, or down a hallway and back. Maybe you are able to take a walk outside, or maybe you are only able to take a few steps within your room. If a walk is not possible, close your eyes and imagine you are taking a walk along a beautiful and picturesque path. Wherever your walk (or imagined walk) takes you, stay in your body during the walk. Spend a few minutes walking. That's all.

SOMETIMES, WE ARE JUST NOT IN CONTROL

As much as we would like to be in control of our lives, we are not. Yes, we can make things happen, we can manifest some of our ideas and dreams, and we can right some wrongs. But there is much that is out of our control. This reality of not being in control is uncomfortable to sit with. For Lydia, the forks and the messiness in her life were out of her control, and she had to sit with that unpredictability. As hard and scary as being out of control is to face, it feels equally hard and scary to sit with in our bodies.

When I rushed to my mom's side as she sat in the emergency room, we learned that a lesion had been found near her pancreas. So many feelings overtook me. Terror, anger, and helplessness swirled inside me. As we sat in the hospital room, waiting was all we could do. The rest was out of our hands, out of our control. I alternated between being up in my head with all my anxious and panicked thoughts and making calls to my family. The waiting was excruciating. I wanted nothing more than to feel in control. But I was not.

When I got into bed that night, my body was screaming at me. Lying in bed, I finally took the time to feel myself.

> *My throat had a dry, chalky coating. My chest was burning and held so tight. My arms ached as if they had held a heavy weight for hours, and a lead lump sat squarely in my heart. My body couldn't sleep, so I lay there in the dark and listened to my body. And felt myself for the first time all day.*

Feeling my felt emotions didn't change the situation, but it did change the power dynamic between me and the unpredictable world, just a bit. Knowing that I could stay with myself in that hard moment gave me a small sense of power in a very powerless moment.

Maybe you recognize a similar moment in your own life when you were

- Waiting for a school or job acceptance

- Waiting to hear about a medical diagnosis or the results of a pathology report
- Waiting for an important response or reply

Letting go of control or the illusion of control is so hard because we are trying to hope something into reality or to change something that cannot be changed. In those moments, we are desperate for our reality to not be our reality. We want something different. These moments can be some of the toughest to navigate because feelings of powerlessness can be excruciating to sit with.

While we don't have control of an unpredictable world, we can feel a glimmer of empowerment in those moments. Empowerment arises from our ability to stay grounded in our bodies, instead of spiraling upwards and out of ourselves. Empowerment grows with the learned confidence that we don't have to flee our bodies when the going gets tough. When faced with challenge and adversity, staying in ourselves and our bodies, even for just a bit, is indeed within our power.

THE FLEETING FIX OF DISCHARGING OUR FEELINGS VS. OWNING THEM

When I say we are responsible for our feelings, I do not simply mean that we must express them in a socially acceptable and responsible way, although that is part of our work, to be sure. To be responsible for our feelings means that we feel them, process them, own them, and move through them so that we liberate them. So that we release the hold that our emotions have on us and the people we love.

I believe that as a society we must learn to feel our difficult and challenging emotions. When we protect our children from their hard feelings, we are not teaching them to survive tough feelings. It is with the best of intentions that we give every child a trophy, both literally and figuratively, but we are not doing our children any favors by not allowing them to feel their disappointment, rejection, and failure. Part of growing up is learning how to get through tough feelings.

We see the result of spewing feelings, displacing them, and discharging them every day. A prime example of this is how we navigate and interact with others online; the ways we respond to social media, as we troll and comment on conversation threads, demonstrate a very stark and unbecoming reality. Being online, we don't need to show our faces or use our real names to spill our opinions and, yes, our emotions out into the world. The way we behave online is emblematic of the problem; we don't have to own our feelings, we are not held responsible for the havoc they wreak, and we get a fleeting fix by the temporary discharge of our emotional confusion, suffering, and pain.

It is vital that we look at this social problem and address it. It is imperative that we remedy this in ourselves and see it as an opportunity to do better and be better. To grow and change. We can be brave and resilient feelers who take ownership of our own feelings. We learn how to own them and feel them, and we embrace the opportunity to do so.

UNDAUNTED BY EMOTION

If we get really good at WELCOME-ing in and outlasting feelings, a very cool thing begins to happen. We begin to live our lives undaunted by our emotions. We make decisions without the fear of failing or making mistakes. We may find ourselves taking more risks or living more adventurously. When we are undaunted by hard emotions, we become more tolerant of life's unpredictability and messiness; we face challenge and adversity with more resilience.

When we know we can withstand feelings of insecurity, failure, embarrassment, or rejection, we no longer decline invitations, turn down opportunities to travel, or purposefully avoid chances to meet new people or try new things. In the face of our social anxiety, shame, or jealousy, we don't blink an eye — not because we no longer feel these feelings, of course we do — but we know we can get through them. To the feelings that may have prompted us to stay home and make excuses, we say, "We got this!" No more being held hostage by our hard feelings.

What we have learned in this book — to stretch our inner containers, to exercise and tend to our feeling muscle, and to WELCOME in feelings — has given us tools. Unbearable feelings can be more bearable. Feelings that were once intolerable can become more tolerable. And bit by bit, we take back pieces of our lives. We can face difficulty and uncertainty with a new confidence — the confidence that if we are embarrassed, if we fail, and if we are rejected, we will survive. We can indeed handle hard feelings.

WE ARE ONLY HUMAN

Opening up to more feeling in your body and your life is a process. It can be a beautiful process, but it is also hard work. You will make gains in your willingness to stay with feelings, and then you will falter at times because you are only human.

I encourage everyone reading this book to embrace a loving kindness towards yourself as you move through this process. If you find yourself falling into an old habit after months of a daily feeling practice, be gentle with yourself. Simply acknowledge and observe where you want to do better or do something differently, and do your best to stay with the practice that you have developed.

Sometimes, an apology can be very meaningful in the moments when you trip up – an apology to yourself and/or to those around you. You cannot always be the person you want to be, but you can always apologize and make a commitment to do better.

Recently, I had a very complicated day, full of feelings of disappointment and inadequacy. Whether these feelings were warranted or justified wasn't the point; they were very real and very powerful within me. And as life would have it, in addition to navigating all my many feelings, I needed to go grocery shopping.

As I was walking the cavernous aisles of Costco, my husband called me with a question. As can happen sometimes, a simple misunderstanding between partners can spark big, big, big feelings. With my container already filled to the brim with inadequacy, I found myself spewing angry feelings in a very loud voice in the middle of one of the oversized frozen food aisles, my voice surely echoing through other nearby sections. While I can usually ride out my "frustrated at my husband" felt emotion – which is a distinct and familiar building energy of what I call "hard bubbles" in my chest – this time, I could not. Not one of my best moments, for sure.

After collecting myself and taking a minute to reflect on my outburst, I apologized to my daughter who was with me, albeit having smartly and quickly taken shelter in another aisle. Later, when I got home, even though I still felt frustration, I apologized to my husband for vomiting my feelings at him. I know better how to communicate my angry feelings, and the way I acted (again, no matter how right and just I felt in feeling them in the moment) was not okay. I also sent a quiet but heartfelt energetic apology out to the Costco customers who were subjected to my unsightly behavior. I am not always my best self, and I can and will do better next time. I can and will do better next time.

Taking responsibility for our feelings is a big ask sometimes, but it is a necessary step in living to our full potential. When we can't hold, feel, or stay with our feelings, they overflow out into the world – a world already drowning in struggles and problems. Remember, if we don't want to feel our feelings, why would anyone else?

Our commitment to bear responsibility for our feelings not only ensures more resilience and greater presence in our own lives but contributes to a healthier dynamic in our relationships with the people we care about. To top it off, think of the example we set for those around us — our friends, our family, our students, and our children. We can model a responsible approach to feeling our feelings that serves the greater good.

We can't take a back seat and assume feeling is something that just happens — something we don't need to think about or even participate in. Even though we may have learned otherwise, feeling is something that we can participate in. We can teach and awaken our bodies — our feeling muscle — to the task of feeling. Our human proclivity to avoid hard feelings means that if we want to feel deeply and freely, we must actively choose the alternative.

Imagine a world where we take responsibility for our own feelings, and as a result, we don't unload stuff that we don't want to feel on others. A world where we do indeed feel uncomfortable, hard emotions and release the emotion by feeling it, not spewing or offloading it.

Imagine our feelings running their course. Imagine letting the steam out of our emotional pressure cooker. Imagine not burdening those around us with outbursts and firestorms of feeling. Imagine being undaunted by hard feelings. Imagine better tolerating the messiness and unpredictability of life.

Imagine being free to feel what lies within you. May you go forth and play in the waves.

CHAPTER NINE EXPERIENTIAL

I. BODY PLAY: "EXPANDING YOUR INNER CONTAINER" VISUALIZATION

You may want to record your voice reading this guided imagery script to play while you are quietly and comfortably resting or meditating. Or simply read the script first and meditate on the words, concepts, or themes.

Begin by finding a comfortable position: sitting, lying on the floor or a mat, resting in a supported manner. Your eyes may be open or closed. Take a few moments to feel your body. Scan your body from head to toe to notice areas of tension, gripping, or holding as well as areas of releasing or softening.

Begin by feeling your body as a whole, head to toe. Visualize your body as a container that holds your organs, cells, muscles, and vessels. Your container holds your blood and your breath. Your container holds your energy. Take a moment and imagine your energy flowing through your body freely and unimpeded. Imagine the borders of your body as soft, elastic, with plenty of give and room to expand.

Take note of any and all feelings within your body. This could be your heartbeat, your inhale or exhale, your stomach grumbling, your jaw clenching, or an anxious twinge in your

chest. Imagine these feelings flowing through your body.
Freely and unimpeded. There is plenty of room for all the
feelings. Again, imagine the borders of your body as soft and
elastic, with plenty of room to expand.

Find an image of something in your memory that brought
you great comfort, ease, or joy. Use the image to generate
a feeling within you of comfort, ease, or joy. Allow this
feeling to fill your body and to reach those soft, elastic
borders. Allow the feeling to expand and to gently and
softly push the borders of your body, so that the feeling is
big within you. Stay with this big feeling for a few minutes.
Stay with the expansion of your borders. Stay with the soft
and pliable container that is your body.

2. BEGIN TO BE AWARE

Notice the moments when you spill or discharge your feelings
on others. Resist the urge to judge or criticize yourself. Try
reflecting on these questions in writing, meditation, or any form
of creative expression.

- Do your feelings overflow your inner container? Does
  your inner container feel full and small? Flexible and
  expandable?
- Do you discharge feelings onto people in your life?
  Colleagues? Friends? Family?
- Do you discharge feelings online?

- Do you know when your container is full? So very full?
- Can you recognize when you have taken responsibility for a tough feeling rather than discharging it? Do you know how to do that? Can you practice and commit to taking responsibility for your feelings?
- Can you own your most difficult feelings and find a way to feel them, bit by bit?

This is big stuff. Hard stuff. But so worthwhile.

3. "OWNING MY FEELINGS" WRITING PROMPT

Use this statement as a springboard for a journal entry, a short story, a painting/picture, a meditation, a poem, a song, a dance, or any form of creative expression.

I am owning my feelings by learning how to stay with them, outlast them, and not discharge them on those I love. An example of this is...

EPILOGUE

I realize that you may have some feelings as this book comes to a close – feelings of validation, acknowledgment, and new insight. But there may be other feelings too – feelings of discomfort, of dissatisfaction, and of untidy resolutions. I admit that is very much intentional.

Yes, the patient stories in this book do not end with everything tied up in a perfect bow. Sure, some of my personal experiences conclude with more questions than answers. Yes, the fact that felt emotion does not always dissipate, but rather shapeshifts, is frustrating and untidy. My insights often end with what might feel like an unsatisfying or possibly inadequate conclusion – "We are only human," "We are a work in progress," or "Two things can be true at the same time."

We humans crave order, satisfying closure, and tidy resolutions, but life does not promise decisive or polished endings. This book is about sitting with uncomfortable feelings, and it seems fitting that some uncomfortable felt emotion may be generated from its pages.

If aspects of this book brought you discomfort or brought forth strong emotions that would make sense. If it felt validating and reassuring that would make sense. If you disagreed with, questioned, or opposed concepts and ideas that I have presented in this book that would make sense.

As I have said before, my work is anecdotal, and I present it as such. I share my experience and insight as a practitioner of bodywork, a shepherd of feelings, a Frequent Feeler myself, and an observer of our human condition, not as a researcher or scientist. While my work is informed by a medical degree, years of private practice, and extensive research and personal experience with mind-body medicine, my ultimate goal is to present and celebrate our bodies as magnificent and complex, and full of elegant wisdom and graceful knowing.

Learning to be with and listen to our bodies is a gift we give ourselves, and that gift overflows with self-awareness and inner confidence. Our bodies are the home we live in, whether we are literally at home or away from home. Creating space to listen to your body's wisdom is both honoring and tending to your home.

Our human experience is both exquisite and fragile, and while much of our world can be studied, quantified, and measured, our emotional life has some questions yet to be answered. I know I am asking you to sit in a gray area, in the unknown, and at times, in an unanswerable space. Yet, if we can tolerate wading into uncharted waters, we may find a thing or two worth noting.

So, as you sit with the messiness of this ending, the only promise I make is that feeling is a process, messy and hard at times and beautiful and elegant at others. It is my great hope that through the pages of this book you have found new insight into your feeling muscle, and that this insight may bring increased self-awareness, self-acceptance, intention, and resilience into your life – and perhaps a greater appreciation that each moment is yet another opportunity to be present with yourself.

May you play with the ideas in this book. Play, practice, and then play some more.

REFERENCES

Aron, Elaine N. *The Highly Sensitive Person: How to Thrive When the World Overwhelms You*. New York, NY: Broadway Books; 1996.

Benson, Herbert. *The Relaxation Response*. New York, NY: HarperCollins Publishers, Inc.; 1975.

Curtis, Jamie Lee. *Today I Feel Silly & Other Moods That Make My Day*. New York, NY: Joanna Colter Books, An Imprint of HarpersCollins Publishers; 1998.

Dandapani. *The Power of Unwavering Focus*. New York, NY: Portfolio / Penguin; 2022.

Gendlin, Eugene T. *Focusing*. New York, NY: Bantam Books; 1978.

Goleman, Daniel. *Emotional Intelligence: Why It Matters More Than IQ*. London: Bloomsbury; 1995.

Johnson, Don Hanlon, editor. *Bone, Breath, & Gesture: Practices of Embodiment*. Berkeley and San Francisco, CA: North Atlantic Books and The California Institute of Integral Studies; 1995.

Kabat-Zinn, Jon. *Wherever You Go, There You Are*. New York, NY: Hyperion; 1994.

Levine, Peter with Ann Frederick. *Waking the Tiger: Healing Trauma*. Berkeley, CA: North Atlantic Books, Huichin, unceded Ohlone land; 1997.

Mayland, Elaine L. *Rosen Method: An Approach to Wholeness and Well-Being Through the Body*. Santa Fe, NM: 52 Stone Press/PenPower; 2015.

Pert, Candace B. *Molecules of Emotion: The Science Behind Mind-Body Medicine*. New York, NY: Touchstone; 1997.

Rosen, Marion with Susan Brenner. *Rosen Method Bodywork: Accessing the Unconscious through Touch*. Berkeley, CA: North Atlantic Books, 2003.

www.ingramcontent.com/pod-product-compliance
Lightning Source LLC
Chambersburg PA
CBHW021709120626
46545CB00004B/1471